THE CHILDREN'S WAR

THE CHILDREN'S WAR

The Second World War through the eyes of the children of Britain

JULIET GARDINER

PORTRAIT

In association with the Imperial War Museum

Abbreviations, money and weights

Copyright © 2005 by Juliet Gardiner

First published in 2005 by Portrait, an imprint of Piatkus Books Ltd, 5 Windmill Street, London W1T 2JA
e-mail: info@piatkus.co.uk

In association with the Imperial War Museum
www.iwm.org.uk

Every effort has been made to identify and acknowledge copyright holders. Any errors or omissions will be rectified in future editions provided that written notification is made to the publisher.

The moral right of the author has been asserted

A catalogue record for this book is available from the British Library

ISBN 0 7499 5067 6

Designed and edited by Compendium Publishing Ltd, First Floor, 43 Frith Street, London W1D 4SA

Set in Bembo and Franklin Gothic

Printed and bound by in Italy by LEGO SpA

Abbreviations

AFS	Auxiliary Fire Service
ARP	Air Raid Precautions
ATS	Auxiliary Territorial Service
BEF	British Expeditionary Force
CORB	Children's Overseas Reception Board
GNTC	Girls' Naval Training Corps
GTC	Girls' Training Corps
JTC	Junior Training Corps
LCC	London County Council
LDV	Local Defence Volunteers (later the Home Guard)
MoH	Medical Officer of Health
NAAFI	Navy, Army and Air Force Institute (providing retail and leisure services to the Armed Forces)
OTC	Officers' Training Corps
RCM	Refugee Children's Movement
WAAF	Women's Auxiliary Air Force
WJAC	Women's Junior Air Corps
WRNS	Women's Royal Naval Service
WVS	Women's Voluntary Service

Money

The English pound (£) contained 20 shillings (s or /), each of 12 pennies (d). (The '£' came from the Latin 'librum' and the 'd' from 'denarius'.) Two shillings and six pence is written as 2/6d; two shillings as 2/-.

A fairly typical wage was around £3 10s to £4 a week (but only 14/- a week for army privates).

Weight

The pound weight (lb) is equal to approximately 0.45 of a kilogramme. It is divided into 16 ounces (oz), each weighing just under 3 grammes.

Contents

Introduction

MEND AND MAKE-DO TO SAVE BUYING NEW

MAKE-DO AND MEND

ISSUED BY THE BOARD OF TRADE

The Children's War is now everyone's war. In this first decade of the twenty-first century, all those who have clear memories of the Second World War are in their mid-sixties at least. It is their memories of those six long years that increasingly encapsulate the story of the Home Front, told in books, radio and television programmes. They pass the stories on to generations who have no personal memory of that time but who are avid to know how it was in the first, though tragically not the last, war that put civilians – children included – centre stage on the battleground that was the Home Front between 1939 and 1945.

Indeed, the first imperative of the war in Britain, along with issuing gas masks and insisting that homes, shops, offices and streets must be blacked out, was the order to 'get the children away' from urban areas where bombs were expected to fall the minute hostilities were declared. From that moment forward, children were inextricably part of both the war experience and the war effort. Almost nothing that affected the civilian population would pass its children by. From ration books to the Blitz, from collecting salvage to recognising that 'it's patriotic to be shabby', children were up there on the front line. Government propaganda recognised this: children's welfare was entwined in the national message. 'Dig for Victory' so that children could have the green vegetables and fruit they needed in wartime; save for war bonds, and thus ensure your child's future; 'Do Without', 'Make Do and Mend', 'Holiday at Home' so that what few scarce resources there were could be diverted for children's well-being.

It was a war almost no one wanted. The enthusiasm that marked the start of the First World War was almost entirely absent. Although appeasement was later stigmatised and the 1930s condemned as a 'low, dishonest decade', historians have recently judged less harshly the desperate search for peace of a nation that was prepared to condone so much in its anxiety to avert another world war. Politicians were well aware how profoundly unprepared the country was for war, and how high the cost of rearmament might be for social stability at home. The people hoped against hope that collective security might ensure world peace, and only reluctantly realised that the price was too high, the demands and violations ultimately unappeasable.

And when it came, the war spared no one, children perhaps least of all. The war wearied and diminished everyone. It went on too long; it killed, injured, bereaved and rent apart too often; socially and culturally it impoverished too many. And children suffered in the myriad ways that adults did, but their loss was compounded by the draining away of their normal expectations of childhood, years that could never be recovered.

The passing of peace. Children stand on sandbags to gaze at a plenitude of toys still on sale in a West End store at Christmas, 1939.

Yet there is invariably a natural resilience in young children, an often surprisingly unquenchable optimism, and children's own accounts of their daily wartime experiences are full of humour and sharp observations, as well as some sadness and pathos. A child's wartime optic is different from that of an adult: it gives a differently refracted view. *The Children's War* tries to recreate that view, telling the story wherever possible in children's own words, drawn either from the letters they wrote and the diaries they kept during the war, or from the vivid memories that those who are now growing old have of the intense years of their wartime childhood. It also aims to revisit a child's experience of war from the drawings children did, the toys they played with, the clothes they wore, the books and comics they read, and the photographic records of their wartime experiences.

Those wartime children are in great demand today. For schools studying the Second World War as part of the national curriculum, they are a 'primary source' as grandparents go into the classroom to share their recollections, and be quizzed by children on their experiences. They are sought out too by authors, radio and television programme makers, and journalists seeking to recapture the extraordinary experience of a time that changed Britain, in many ways for ever, and played a large part in shaping and defining what it is today.

'Get the children away'

David Eliades, a six-year-old evacuee from London, in September 1939. Around his neck is his gas mask.

'**D**ear Editor,' wrote 13-year-old Elizabeth Mossman to the *News Chronicle* in a competition for 'the 50 best' letters from evacuees telling their own stories of the mass exodus from cities all over Britain on the eve of the Second World War:

I'm sure it was a surprise for all us evacuees to find ourselves scattered about the country, taken to a new home and getting to know our new foster mothers and fathers. At first it was just like another holiday, but after a time a funny feeling of homesickness seemed to creep into me, and I hoped and prayed that the war would end. But it was no use feeling down-hearted, and if we evacuees do stay out of London, I'm sure we will be doing our bit for the country as well as helping the government.

No wonder Elizabeth, who had been evacuated from her home in Streatham, south-west London, to West Wittering near Chichester in Sussex, won a prize: her letter, written on lined notepaper in a clear, rounded hand, perfectly encapsulated the reality of the experience of thousands of evacuees – while at the same time echoing the government's message to parents to send their children out of the cities to what it was hoped would be the safety of the countryside.

The experience of the First World War, when bombs had killed 1,413 civilians and seriously injured a further 3,407, was a spectre that haunted the British government as peace began to crumble in the late 1930s. Military experts calculated that, with Germany's massive rearmament programme and technologically sophisticated aircraft, the toll would be much heavier in another war – and the raids on Barcelona, Madrid, Guernica and other towns and cities during the Spanish Civil War seemed to add substance to this fear. As defence plans began to be put into operation, people remembered the warning of the future Prime Minister Stanley Baldwin back in 1932 that 'the bomber will always get through. I think it is as well for the man in the street to realise that there is no power on earth that can stop him being killed.'

Britain was particularly vulnerable: of the island's population of around 48 million, almost half was concentrated into just the six largest urban conglomerations. Given their key industrial, transport and communication functions, it was reasoned that the populations of these cities would be under constant air attack as soon as war broke out. Some 9 million people, around a fifth of the population, could be expected to be the target of a 'knock-out blow' from the air the moment war was declared. If the attack lasted for 60 days, as many as 600,000 would be killed and 1,200,000 seriously injured. Panic would ensue in the devastation, with thousands seeking shelter or fleeing the

Los Niños

Among the first of hundreds and thousands of refugee children who would come to Britain from Europe before, during and after the Second World War were nearly 4,000 Basque children who sailed into Southampton aboard an old cruise liner, the SS Habana, on 23 May 1937. They were refugees from the Nationalist bombing of Durango, Guernica and Bilbao during the Spanish Civil War when nationalist forces under the command of General Franco fought to overthrow the democratically elected Republican government.

Although individuals – including George Orwell – went to fight for the Republican cause, the British government was anxious that the war should not escalate into a Europe-wide conflict. While troops and military equipment from Hitler's Germany and Mussolini's Italy poured in to help Franco, and Russian arms and equipment arrived to aid the Republic, Britain maintained a policy of non-intervention.

The evacuation of the Basque children was arranged by the National Joint Committee for Spanish Relief, a voluntary organisation representing all political opinion and none, and camps and hostels – colonies as they were known – were set up all over Britain for the refugees. 'Sólo por tres meses', the children were told, 'it'll only be for three months', since it was hoped that by then the battle for northern Spain would be over. In the event most of the refugees remained in Britain for nearly two years, and some 250 were never able to return to their homeland.

carnage. People – particularly those in the poorer areas – would have 'an almost irresistible impulse to get out or bolt,' predicted the chairman of a committee set up in 1931 to consider the problem of civil defence in case of war. The solution must be to move as many people as possible away from the cities in an orderly fashion before the bombers came, MPs argued when the first Air Raid Precautions Bill came before Parliament in late 1937. It would be impossible to construct sufficient shelters for the entire civilian population of Britain's major cities: as many as possible must leave.

The Munich crisis in September 1938 was the first test of the government's evacuation scheme. The London County Council (LCC) drew up tentative plans for the evacuation of some 637,000 children from London, and there were hastily improvised plans to move children out of Birmingham and other areas. In the event, 1,200 nursery school children and 3,100 children classed as 'physically defective' were moved from London.

The headmistress of the Mary Datchelor School in Camberwell, Dr (later Dame Dorothy) Brock, had roped in the girls of the Secretarial Sixth Form to type up notices

9

War comes home. Corrugated steel Anderson shelters are delivered to householders in Muswell Hill, north London, for erection in the back garden.

inviting parents to the school to discuss the grave situation. The school hall was crammed on the night of the meeting, Monday 26 September 1938, as she outlined:

> the Government Scheme for 'School Migration' … plans for getting the children away if a 'State of Emergency' were announced on the wireless, plans for keeping the boys and girls in a family together, plans about luggage, plans for putting up a notice on the school gates to let parents know where we were sent, plans for billets, and plans for working with local schools and for keeping as normal a school life going as possible.

From that night Dr Brock and her staff 'lived in an atmosphere of lists, labels and luggage', and by Wednesday 28 September 'our party numbered between 600 and 700.

Things looked very black.' But tension eased when it appeared that Hitler and Chamberlain had come to an agreement over the dismemberment of Czechoslovakia, war was averted, and on 30 September Chamberlain was able to promise 'peace for our time' to the British people. The Mary Datchelor staff 'filed lists, labels [were] put away and luggage taken home. Normal school life began again,' and the 4,000-odd special needs children who had been sent out of London were brought back again. But one Mary Datchelor pupil at least was disappointed: in an article for the school magazine on 'The School Evakuashn' she wrote, 'On Wednesday they said we would go on Thursday. On Thursday we went to School and they said we were not going. I was really sorry, I did want to go for one afternoon.' But when the school finally was evacuated nearly 12 months later, it would be for almost six long years.

The crisis had shown just how much work still needed to be done: while thousands of children from London's East End were to be evacuated to parts of Essex, the Essex Education Board was preparing to evacuate its children from those very areas, and as the independent King's School, Canterbury, was evacuating its pupils to the safety of Scotland, the LCC took over the school's buildings for evacuees from London.

Over the next few months as the clouds of war grew darker, work on 'Operation Pied Piper', the code name for the evacuation of children, got under way in earnest. The Ministry of Health and the Board of Education were charged with the task, since the welfare and schooling of children would be crucial aspects of any evacuation. The scheme was a government one, aimed largely at poorer parts of the community where people would have neither the resources nor the contacts to send their children to a place of safety. There was no reason why families who could send their children to stay with relatives or friends in the country should not make their own arrangements, and thousands did. Independent fee-paying schools likewise scoured Britain for suitable places where their pupils could continue their education in areas they hoped would be far away from the ravages of war.

The country was divided into three categories: evacuation areas, invariably industrial towns and cities and the areas round military installations, which were soon known as 'danger zones'; 'neutral areas', which children would neither be sent to nor evacuated from; and 'reception areas', rural or coastal towns and villages designated to receive evacuees. Ominously, while 200 local authorities that had been ranked as reception areas petitioned to be reclassified as neutral, no authority asked to be a reception area. The main areas to be evacuated were metropolitan London and what is now Greater London; the Medway ports (Chatham, Rochester and Gillingham); the south coast ports of Southampton, Portsmouth and Gosport; industrial areas in the Midlands such as Birmingham, Coventry, Derby and Nottingham; Merseyside (Liverpool, Bootle, Wallasey, Birkenhead, Manchester and Salford); industrial towns in Yorkshire like Bradford, Leeds, Sheffield, Grimsby and Middlesbrough; Newcastle, Gateshead, South Shields, Jarrow and similar ports on the north-east coast; and Glasgow, Edinburgh, Dundee, Clydebank and the Rosyth area of Dunfermline in Scotland.

There would be four categories of evacuees: the blind and disabled; pregnant women; mothers with babies and/or pre-school-age children, who would be evacuated with them;

MOTHERS Send them out of London

Give them a chance of greater safety and health

11

The government had sent parents in the so-called 'danger zones' a leaflet before war broke out urging that they should register their children for the official evacuation scheme, and later would reinforce the message and the strictures about gas masks with posters like this.

TAKE YOUR GAS MASK EVERYWHERE

Kindertransport

Kristallnacht, 'night of the broken glass', 9 November 1938, when the streets of German towns and cities crunched with the shattered glass from Jewish shops and businesses while synagogues burned, pricked the conscience of the world about the plight of the Jews in Nazi Germany. After Hitler came to power as Chancellor in January 1933, he had promulgated a torrent of anti-Jewish laws, stripping German Jews of their civil, cultural and economic rights, closing their businesses, ransacking their homes and evicting them, all in pursuit of the Führer's aim of a 'racially pure' Germany, ridding the German Volk of alien elements.

12

It was clear to the Jews that they had no future in Germany – or Austria either, which had been annexed by Hitler in March 1938. Intense pressure was put on them to leave. But Jews could only leave if they had somewhere to go and, in the grip of worldwide economic recession – and often with strong currents of anti-Semitism within their own countries – Western Europe (including Britain), North America and Australasia would agree to take only a small percentage of Jewish refugees.

But the violence of Kristallnacht 'horrified' the British Prime Minister, Neville Chamberlain, and his government agreed that Britain would accept an unspecified number of Jewish children aged between 5 and 17. However, strict conditions were placed

on this humanitarian gesture. The various British refugee agencies guaranteed that they would bear all the costs and the Kinder would not be a charge on the British taxpayer, their stay was to be strictly temporary, and a £50 bond had to be posted for each child 'to assure their ultimate resettlement' elsewhere.

The Movement for the Care of Children in Germany, later called the Refugee Children's Movement (RCM), sent representatives to Germany and Austria to organise the selection, processing and transportation of the children. Priority was given to those who were in greatest

danger: teenagers already in concentration camps or who had parents in the camps; children in Jewish orphanages or those whose parents, stripped of their livelihoods, could no longer support them; and children threatened with deportation. Meanwhile in Britain an appeal was made for families to provide homes for the refugees.

The first Kindertransport left Berlin on 1 December and Vienna on 10 December 1938. Germany had insisted that the Jewish exodus should not use their ports so the trains travelled through the Netherlands, and at the Hook of Holland the children boarded a ferry that took them to Harwich or Southampton. Eventually some 10,000 children arrived in Britain.

Most British hosts preferred to take in young children, but teenagers, who were most at risk, were brought out first. Unless arrangements had already been made for them to stay with family or friends, they had to be accommodated in freezing cold camps in East Anglia where hundreds were crammed together, a chaotic mix of teenagers and young children from very different backgrounds.

'Cattle markets' were held every week and would-be foster parents 'chose' a refugee to go and live with them. Not all of these were suited to their roles and young Jews could be treated cruelly, sexually abused or set to work as skivvies.

The last Kindertransport left Germany on 1 September 1939 just two days before war was declared. Those who were already in Britain shared the native experience of internal evacuation, some welcomed into comfortable homes while others were isolated in rural areas with no understanding of their needs and practices, or continued to live in hostels or work on farms. In June 1940, over 1,000 of those aged 16 or over who had come with the Kindertransport were detained and joined other so-called 'enemy aliens' in internment camps – despite the fact that they had come to Britain because they were fleeing from the 'enemy'.

For those who had come to Britain on the Kindertransport, it was the chance of a safe – if not always entirely satisfactory – new life. But almost all would never again see the parents they had left behind again. They too would be orphans of the Holocaust.

13

Above: Jewish Kindertransport refugees in a British camp in 1938.

Left: Teenage Jewish girls go through British customs at Harwich, 2 December 1938.

and school-age children, who would be evacuated with their schools. (In Scotland all children were evacuated with their mothers rather than as schools with their teachers.) The evacuation of children was never made compulsory (though such a step was sometimes contemplated) and this made it much harder for the authorities to make accurate forecasts, but they predicted that overall some 4 million people would require evacuation – more than half the total population of Australia at the time – and of those, 1,400,000 were to be evacuated from the greater London area. Children were to be billeted in private homes with 'foster parents' rather than in specially built hostels, which were considered too expensive and would not provide a homely atmosphere for the evacuees. In any case there was simply not enough time to build a vast network of camps in rural areas, though some 50 camps housing around 300 children each were built for 'difficult' evacuees who were hard to place in private homes and for homeless refugees from abroad. Still, 90 per cent of the evacuees would have to be found billets in private houses, and in February 1939 local authorities started on the massive task of finding exactly how much accommodation was available in the reception areas. How many householders would be prepared to take children or mothers and babies into their homes?

When all the returns were in, it was revealed that there was suitable accommodation throughout the country for around 4,800,000 evacuees. But this was overoptimistic. By the end of February 1939 the number was going down steadily as householders in the reception areas claimed that they no longer had any surplus accommodation, since they had agreed to take in family and friends in the event of war rather than have an unknown urban child land on their doorstep. The government felt it could do little to prevent householders from taking in whoever they wished in the event of war: all it could do was use moral suasion exercised through local authorities in the reception areas.

'Albany Road evacuated 11 a.m.,' wrote Miss Dorothy Hoyles, the headmistress of the Camberwell elementary school, in the School Log on 1 September 1939, the day that Hitler's troops marched into Poland. It all seemed to go like clockwork. The 204 children clambered into four trams at 11.25 a.m. These dropped them outside the Old Vic theatre, from where they were marched across the road to Waterloo station to board a train that left at 12.30 p.m. Exactly three hours later the train pulled into Wareham station in Dorset, where the children 'left the train, passed through [the] medical tent (no casualties to report) received cups of tea and biscuits, boarded 'buses and were brought to Central School, Weymouth where they were billeted in private houses. Billeting lasted from 5.30–11 p.m.' But not many evacuations were so apparently trouble-free as this one.

Teachers had been summarily recalled from their summer holidays on 24 August 1939 and since then had been frantically putting the final touches to the arrangements to evacuate their schools. Back in July, as schools were breaking up for the summer holidays, *Public Information Leaflet No. 3. Evacuation Why and How?* had been pushed through every letterbox in the country. 'There are still a number of people who ask "What is the need for all this business about evacuation? Surely if war comes it would be better for families to stick together and not go breaking up their homes?"' The leaflet explained that while this was an understandable feeling, the threat of 'determined attacks from the air' meant that:

Gas masks

By September 1939, 44 million gas masks, or 'respirators' as they were officially called, had been distributed to the British public in the expectation that the Germans would use poison gas. ARP wardens were issued with large, football-match style rattles to sound in the event of a gas attack, which fortunately never came.

Government posters warned, 'Hitler will send no warning – so always carry your gas mask,' though it was never compulsory to do so, and by November 1939 a survey revealed that only 24 per cent of men and 39 per cent of women in London were carrying their masks.

Children between two and five were issued with 'Mickey Mouse' gas masks (below left

and above right) that sported a strange red protuberance and had blue rims round the eyes. This was supposed to make putting them on seem like dressing up rather than Civil Defence.

Babies of course presented particular problems. At first, all a mother could do was wrap her baby tightly in a blanket, but by late October 1939 infants under two were supplied with a 'baby bag', which was a bit like a haversack with a Perspex visor (below right). 'You slid the baby in and then sealed it, and the mothers had to keep pumping on the bellows to get the air in. Oh, there were a lot of tears seeing these babes-in-arms in gas masks,' remembers Harold Shipley, a 14-year old who helped fit them in Hull.

15

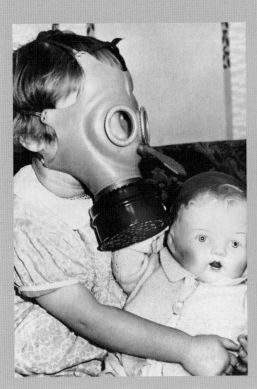

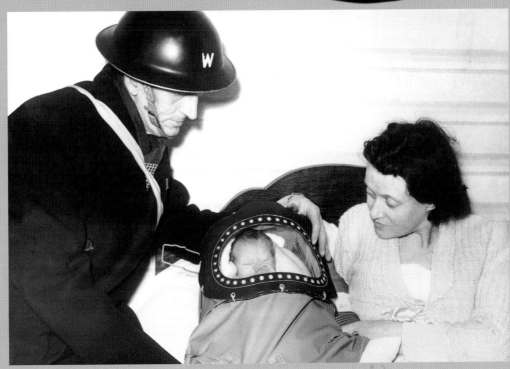

We must see to it that the enemy does not secure his chief objectives – the creation of anything like panic, or the crippling dislocation of our civil life. *One of the first measures we can take to prevent this is the removal of the children from the more dangerous areas.* The scheme is entirely a voluntary one, but clearly the children will be much safer and happier away from the big cities where the dangers will be greatest. There is room in the safer areas for these children; householders have volunteered to provide it. They have offered homes where the children will be made welcome. The children will have their schoolteachers and other helpers with them and their schooling will be continued.

Parents who had not already registered their children for evacuation were encouraged to do so, even though 'it means heartache to be separated from your children' and were warned to think the matter '*over carefully and think of your child or children in good time.* Once air attacks have begun it might be very difficult to arrange to get away.'

Despite official urgings, many parents were reluctant to send their children away, concerned for their safety but nevertheless convinced that it would be better for the family to stick together in perilous times. 'If we're going to be bombed, we'll all stay here together and be bombed together' was an oft-heard mantra. In Birkenhead:

'Though many parents had stated as long as six months ago that they wished their children to be evacuated, they suddenly changed their mind on Monday [at an evacuation practice] and decided not to let them go away. On the other hand, there were those parents who at the last minute said they wanted their children evacuated, thus adding to the general confusion.'

Some families were reluctant to evacuate older children because they were needed at home to help around the house by looking after younger siblings or doing odd jobs, particularly if a husband was likely to be called up into the forces, or to supplement the meagre family income by going out to work if they were 14, the school-leaving age.

Irene Weller's mother was very equivocal about letting her and her brothers be evacuated from Small Heath, Birmingham:

'She was a widow so she hadn't got anyone to discuss it with. Neighbours influenced her I think. They pointed out that there

East End children clutching their gas masks and worldly possessions in shoe bags and pillow cases, make their way to the station en route for evacuation to the country on 2 September 1939.

16

were a lot of factories in the area, Dunlop for example. After all, Birmingham was a big industrial centre. It was only natural that it would be a target. We were quite near the BSA [Birmingham Small Arms factory] and there was a railway station and the ARP [Air Raid Precautions] warden warned that the bombers would make straight for these factories – they'd be number one targets. And my mother would say, "Mrs So and So said this, and then Mr So and So advised that," and it just went on and on, round and round. And my mother would put her head in her hands sometimes and weep. ... It was a very big decision to make – and no one to discuss it with, with my Dad dead and my brother gone into the Army. And another neighbour said, "When the sirens go and we have to run to the shelters I've only got one to run with and the baby, but you've got another four."

The reality of evacuation. Mothers, who were not allowed on the station platform, strain to catch a glimpse of their children setting off from Waterloo station for an unknown destination.

18

A policeman bends down to inspect the label of a small evacuee while the nun in charge of the children looks on. The boy on the right carries his belongings tied up in a brown paper parcel rather than the haversack that was recommended.

And by this time there were ARP centres popping up all over the place. And different buildings had been commandeered for different purposes. I remember going along to the swimming baths one day and finding them shut and a notice saying "Men Contaminated" and "Women Contaminated", and people found that very frightening. I think that's what decided my Mum to send us really.'

Some schools had been holding dress rehearsals for evacuation since the early summer, assembling children in the playground, marching them crocodile-style accompanied by teachers to the railway station, and then marching back again. Now the pace quickened. On 28 August children who were still on holiday were recalled to their school for a practice; each morning they would leave home and parents, unsure whether they would be returning home at teatime or if this was evacuation day. Stanley Reed, a teacher at an

East End school, remembered it as:

> a twilight period. … School had a holiday atmosphere, as though it were the end of term instead of the beginning of a new school year. I abandoned teaching conventional subjects and we spent the days in endless talks, about God, politics, tiddler-fishing and the techniques of pilfering from stalls in the market.

On 31 August 1939 the anticipated order came from the Ministry of Health: 'Evacuate Forthwith', though it was stressed that 'no one should conclude that war is now inevitable'. In the early hours of Friday 1 September, the massive exercise 'to get the children away' began. For Irene Weller:

> 1st September was the worst day of the war, far worse than anything that came later. … My mother kept polishing our shoes. She kept saying, 'We must get these polished, it's very important.' I suppose it gave her something to do, to stop crying. And she kept keep going over the list of things we had to take. Toothpaste, toothbrushes. And of course, being poor, we only had one tube of toothpaste between the four of us, and she kept saying, 'I don't know how you are going to manage if you're split up. I just don't know.'

As instructed, children assembled in their school playgrounds as early as 6.30 a.m. clutching knapsacks, suitcases, pillowcases, carrier bags or even brown paper parcels containing as much as their parents had been able to provide from the list they had received from the government. This instructed them that their child should be evacuated with 'a child's gas mask, a change of underclothing, night clothes, house shoes or plimsolls, spare stockings or socks, a toothbrush, a comb, towel, soap and face cloth, handkerchiefs; and, if possible, a warm coat or mackintosh'. But even this fairly basic list taxed the resources of many families from deprived inner-city areas – the very places from which the majority of the children taking part in the official government evacuation scheme came. A Tynemouth schoolteacher was impressed, however, when she examined the luggage of the children from her school:

> to see if they had the full complement of articles mentioned in the list. …The School … was in one of the poorer districts, and I was surprised by the thoroughness most mothers had displayed in equipping their children. In a batch of 20 in the room where I was working, only one family of four had not all the listed articles. Their mother, who was shabby and looked undernourished, said she intended to buy them that day, and the teacher in charge could look at their luggage the following morning. About half out of the 20 had brand new pyjamas, new soap, new toothbrushes, new plimsolls, new shirts for the boys and new knickers for the girls. A teacher told me that one of the mothers would be paying for her children's new clothes till Christmas.

The reality of evacuation. A child from Chatham in Kent (above) **is overwhelmed by the enormity of being sent away for her own safety to live with strangers in a place far from home. Meanwhile, another, unidentified child** (below) **seems less concerned – indicating, perhaps, that she was under school age and therefore travelling with her mother.**

19

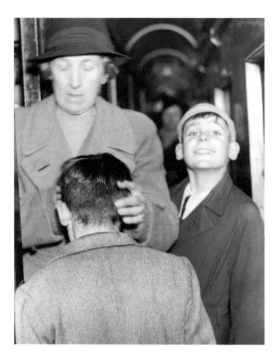

Verminous heads? A doctor checks an evacuee for nits in the corridor of a train as it heads towards a reception area.

20

CARROTS
keep you healthy and help you
to see in the blackout

Mothers were also advised to provide their children with sustenance for the journey: sandwiches, cheese, fruit, raisins and barley sugar (not chocolate) were recommended. Some of the smaller children clutched a much-loved soft toy and clung onto it as a link with home; others were carrying wooden trains, while the older ones might have made provision for the journey with a bundle of thumbed and grimy favourite comics or a book. The children, as instructed, carried their gas masks in cardboard containers slung on cords over their shoulders, the sharp edges banging their knees as they walked. In the school yard, luggage labels would be tied onto their coats giving their names and the number allocated to their school. But no destination: parents would not know where their children had gone until they received a stamped postcard that had been given to each child with instructions to send it home as soon as they arrived at their destination, to tell their parents that they were safe – and where they were.

Irene Weller (now Mead) remembers how:

> All the mothers were stood on their doorsteps crying as we walked to the station, and I said to my brothers as we walked past our house, 'don't look round whatever you do,' because I knew my mum would be there waving. So we just looked straight ahead and when we got past I looked at my brothers and they were still looking straight ahead like I'd told them to but tears were just pouring down all our faces.
>
> Once we'd turned the corner it wasn't so bad, and when we got on the train at Bordsley station we sat together as a family and because I was the oldest I just held onto them, the three of us – the youngest who was only five stayed at home with our mother – we all hung together and that's how we went through everything that happened to us in the war, holding together like that.

'I want to stop with you. I want to get killed with you,' Rose Kops had screamed to her mother as she assembled in the Stepney school playground with her older brother Bernard and the other pupils, 'with our gas masks and labels tied to our coats. And then we all moved away, all the children and the parents crying.' Twelve-year-old Bernard Kops felt a mixture of fear and excitement – and was aware that:

> For my mother the separation from us was even worse than the thought of war.
>
> We marched away crocodile fashion and I looked back at Stepney Green. The leaves so green in the September sunlight. This was the place where we were born, where we grew up, where we played and sang, laughed and cried. And now the grey faces we passed were all weeping. It was strangely quiet. Only the birds in the trees were singing now. They didn't know about the crisis. They didn't know what man was bringing to earth.

Most children were marched onto buses, coaches, the underground or local trains, or piled into commandeered taxis and cars from the 1,589 assembly points in London en route for one of the capital's 168 'entraining stations': main line termini and suburban

Blackout

'Is your blackout really black?' trilled the words of a popular wartime song, and householders spent many tiresome hours ensuring that not a chink of light could be seen glinting though a crack in their curtains. If it was, an ARP warden was likely to yell 'put that light out,' and fines could be salutary. Children were frequently put in charge of ensuring that their family's blackout was in place half an hour after sunset every evening, and reminded to undress in the dark if there was no blackout at their bedroom windows.

In the streets the blackout made life hazardous. Street lights were all but obliterated, traffic lights shielded, and car headlights had to be covered so that only a tiny crescent of light showed. In the first six months of the war 4,133 people were killed on Britain's roads, and of those 2,657 were pedestrians – including large numbers of children. Kerb stones and tree trunks were painted white, as were car bumpers and bicycle mudguards, and anxious mothers tucked white handkerchiefs into their children's pockets, painted their satchels white, and urged them to carry a torch (though this had be covered in tissue paper and the light directed downwards – and soon it was nearly impossible to buy replacement batteries anyway).

21

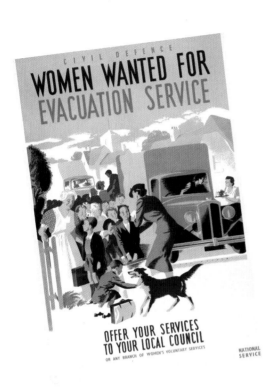

Right: London brother and sister evacuees, Tony and June Bryant, wait to be allocated to foster homes. The luggage label June wore to identify her and the school she was with, got mixed up with that of another girl in the same party. Tony would marry that girl many years later.

22

stations in outer London such as Ealing Broadway, Richmond or New Cross Gate from which the evacuees would depart for the country. It was much the same in danger zones all over the country as the 'great trek' as the Minister of Health called it, 'an exodus bigger than that of Moses', equivalent to the 'movement of ten armies', got under way. Some evacuees went by boat: Betty Smith was one of those who was conveyed by pleasure boat down the Thames from Tilbury in Essex on a trip to Yarmouth that lasted five hours, and some Scottish schoolchildren made their exit from Glasgow, nosing down the Clyde in boats painted battleship grey with the portholes covered over.

Parents of the majority of evacuees who travelled by train were not allowed onto the platform. For Dr Brock, the headmistress of Mary Datchelor School:

> one of the pictures I will always keep in my mind is our last view of the mothers and fathers waving through the railings above the station as we waved goodbye while the train steamed out of London. We had their children in trust, and to keep life as normal and safe and happy for them as possible was our task. As we went, the balloon barrages were slowly rising all round us – a strangely beautiful sight, and a dramatic reminder of the reasons for our going.

Since fear of impending air raids was what gave the evacuation exercise its pressing urgency, plans had concentrated on the logistics of getting the children away from congested urban areas as quickly as possible rather than on how they would be dealt with once they arrived at their destination. It had been anticipated that 3.5 million would need to be got away in the three days scheduled for the evacuation. In the event the number was nearer to 1.9 million, though this shortfall was not admitted at the time. The reasons were not obvious and varied greatly from region to region. On the whole, those with a large number of children were more prepared for at least some of their offspring to be evacuated than were those families with an only child, and local customs of childcare may have played a part. It was suggested that children were more likely to be sent from very deprived areas where parents were more used to obeying 'authority' without too many questions, but in general it seemed that in places such as Merseyside, where preparations were very thorough and parents were consulted whenever possible, they were more ready to accept that evacuation was in their children's best interest. Overall, fewer than half the schoolchildren in English towns and cities (including London) were evacuated, and 38 per cent were moved from evacuation areas in Scotland.

It might be thought that having fewer children to move would make the operation more efficient, but this was not the case. Since it made no sense for trains and coaches to set off half-empty, they were filled up with whatever evacuees presented themselves – school parties, mothers and babies, pregnant women – regardless of their destination.

For some children, many of whom had never been on a train before, it was all a big adventure, and not knowing where they were going added to the thrill. This is how newspapers and newsreels portrayed the evacuees. Bernard Kops, who would grow up to be a playwright, 'could hardly contain myself with excitement when [the train] moved out of the station. I jumped from window to window.' But then he:

came back to earth with a clunk when I looked at my terrible responsibility, my crying, snotty-nosed red-eyed little sister. I had promised to look after her and not be separated from her. 'But where will we be tonight?' she appealed to me. And I shrugged. 'Your guess is as good as mine.' 'But we'll be with strangers.' Rose had never been away from home, never been more than six inches away from my mother, and now she was clinging onto me and the other children were watching.

And as the train carrying Hilda Cooper 'pulled out of the station, the crying started and some children were so upset they were physically sick. I remember thinking, "Please make it go away. I don't want this adventure. I want my mum."'

Bernard and Rose Kops were bound for Denham in Buckinghamshire – 'where the film studios are' – only 20 miles from London and within two miles of the Metropolitan underground at Uxbridge, but Hilda Cooper's destination was North Wales, and other children were heading for places that were hundreds of miles from home. Barbara Wilson recalls that:

> It was a long train journey [from Birkenhead to Harlech] and there were no toilets on the train. The teachers realised that the children couldn't have drinks so they gave us bags of … fruit drops and they taught us to sing 'Men of Harlech'.

By the time the train pulled into a station in Kent, 13-year-old Hazel Brown was exhausted. Early that morning her school had assembled at Mary Datchelor in Camberwell, south London.

> [We] crocodiled out of the school gates, youngest children in front to set the pace for the 20-minute climb up the hill to Denmark Hill station. … Once at the station we were counted to the platform, counted into the train and told very firmly to sit down and on no account to open the doors. This was the age of steam so when at last we set off it was rattling and clattering along, clouds of steam blowing back as we lurched to an unknown destination. We ate anything we had left in our bags, that didn't take long, and soon got hot and sticky and tired. Hours later it seemed, we pulled up at a wayside station. We could get out and stretch our legs. The sign said Charing. But this was definitely not Charing Cross. Where were we?
>
> Once again we were lined up and counted and marched off through a village street to a village hall. A committee of local ladies under a billeting officer was waiting. Starting with the youngest and then with families, our names were called out and we were allocated to a household. As we left the Hall to walk away we were given a tin of condensed milk and a tin of corned beef to be passed on to foster mothers. I had never eaten corned beef before. As the hall emptied, our friends being collected by waiting ladies, three of us tried desperately to stay together, difficult since few were prepared to take in more than one or two. Elinor, Gwen and I were the last and it was dusk. Finally a voice said 'I'll take them.' We were pleased but too tired for words. We were taken to a lovely country house in

'Evacuation Day' linocut from the school magazine of Portsmouth Southern Secondary School for Girls which was evacuated to Salisbury on 1 September 1939.

25

huge grounds, taken into the kitchen while upstairs we could hear furniture being moved. I think I fell asleep quickly.

Dorothy King was 11 years old when she was evacuated from her school in Abbey Wood, south London. When the train arrived at Maidstone in Kent, the children were:

bussed out to a church hall where WVS ladies [Women's Voluntary Service members whose 'war task number one' was to travel with parties of evacuees and help in getting them settled] were ready to escort us in groups round the nearby streets, allocating them to the houses on their lists. I doubt if [Mr and Mrs] Merrifield had a reassuring impression of me when I arrived: a plain, bespectacled child. For my part I was horrified at the prospect of being thrown into a house with strange children. ... However only one of two faces [pressed to the window] belonged to the young Merrifields; other spectators were the neighbour's children who happened to be in the house watching the novel proceedings. I was ushered in, the children ushered off, and Mrs Merrifield sat me down alone in the dining

The welcome. Evacuees arrive in Cheltenham where they are met by members of the WVS with cups of tea and buns, before being taken on to their billets in the Cotswolds.

room with a plate of cold meat which I could barely begin to tackle. I was hot, thirsty and desolate! I think that I'd suddenly realised that I had really left home.

Miss Helliar, escorting 30 young children from her school in Stoke Newington in north London, arrived by train in Stevenage in Hertfordshire and then travelled several miles by bus to the village of Kimpton, where they were given a warm welcome by the vicar and some of his parishioners before being sent on to their final destination, Peter's Green. A table was brought out from the village pub and set up on the village green and Betty Helliar sat at it sorting out the billets for 'her' children.

This was quickly done. The children were dog tired and ready for bed and they went off happily with their new 'Aunties'. As they said goodbye to me I stressed that I would be on the village green the next morning in case anyone wanted to talk. Then I set to work on the postcards to the parents and got them safely posted. By this time I was dog tired. It was time for my escort helper and myself to be billeted. … We felt very sorry for people kindly taking in complete strangers and we also felt very sorry for the children going into strange homes.

A cartoon by Giles of the Sunday Express on the evacuation of London schoolchildren to the country.

Not all arrivals were so orderly. Because of the rush to get the children away, many were on the 'wrong' trains and arrived in places where they were not expected. Anglesey in Wales had been expecting 625 elementary school children; in the event 2,468 arrived. Pwllheli, which had not been expecting any evacuees, was informed that 890 were heading their way, though in the event only around half that number detrained at the Welsh resort. A small Norfolk village that had been expecting a contingent of schoolchildren with their teachers found itself host to evacuated mothers and babies from Hoxton and Shoreditch in London's East End. So many more children arrived in Suffolk from Dagenham than had been expected that no billets could be found for them and some had to be

"Now I want you to promise me you're all going to be really good little evacuees and not worry his Lordship."

put up in temporary accommodation without bedding or blankets. As Dorothy King had noted, the headmistress, Dr Brock, and her Mary Datchelor School party:

> arrived intact at a destination, but it was not, unfortunately the right one. We were detrained at Charing, a lovely Kentish village and were sent off in motor buses to Charing Heath, Little Chart, Westwell, Cowlees Farm, Great Chart, Hothfield and Kingsnorth – places as attractive as their names but scattered over a wide area, offering no possibility of carrying on secondary education (since in Kent the education of all children over 11 is centralised in towns), and with no place where we could have any Headquarters and from which the School could be organised, and no place in which it could ever assemble. We later learnt that the Authority was expecting seven elementary schools. [Dr Brock found some days later that her school should have been sent to Ashford and 'rumour says that the train we were to have come on … arrived at Ashford empty, except for the fireman, driver and guard, and went in a circle back to London.'] I have had few worse hours in my life than those I spent watching the School being taken off in drizzling rain and gathering gloom to those unknown villages, knowing, as I did, that I was powerless to do anything about it.

Mothers and under school-aged children who joined the evacuation scheme are served tea by a local Girl Guide.

27

Indeed, as the official historian of the evacuation, Richard L. Titmuss, explains:

> Many reports testify to the general confusion and unpreparedness which characterised the reception of the mothers and children in September 1939. All the troubles caused by lack of pre-knowledge about the evacuees, train delays, the ban on spending [by local authorities in the reception areas] and other factors, were piled higher when many of the parties, travelling in crowded trains, sometimes without lavatories and adequate water supplies, arrived in a dirty and unco-operative state. It was not a good start. Town and country met each other in a critical mood.

The wartime guests were further aggrieved when, in many areas, they were

WEYMOUTH, Sept. 1939

World-War II.
London Schools' Evacuation.

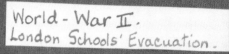

28

Albany Road (J.M.) School, S.E.5.

walked or paraded round while householders took their pick. 'Scenes reminiscent of a cross between an early Roman slave market and Selfridges bargain basement ensued,' one of those in charge of the evacuation of West Hartlepool's schoolchildren complained.

Susan Waters, a 21-year-old teacher who was in charge of a party of small children from Walthamstow in north London, was appalled when after arriving in Bedford, the children were taken by bus to a nearby village:

> The scene was more akin to a cattle or slave market than anything else. The prospective foster mothers, who should not have been allowed onto the field at all, just invaded us and walked about the field picking out what they considered to be the most presentable specimens and then harassed the poor billeting officer for the registration slips if they were to get the necessary cash for food and lodging from the government. Thus it was some hours before the children were all disposed of and those that felt they were going to be left behind were dissolved in tears and hadn't the slightest idea where they were going.

Some women would specify 'two fair-haired, blue-eyed little girls,' while farmers might size up boys to see if they were strong enough to work on the farm. John Wills from Battersea reckoned that:

> If you were similar to Shirley Temple you were grabbed right away. The little angelic girls went first into the homes of who knows what or where. Perhaps some were chosen by the local child molester. But most girls went into the best homes. In the event, if you were like me or my friend Alfie, who always looked even filthier than I did, your chances were pretty bleak.

'If they wanted someone to help around the house, they'd choose a girl and if they wanted help in the garden, then they'd choose a boy,' remembered Reginald Baker, whose father 'drove one of the last Royal Mail vans to use a horse' and 'liked his drink. In the East End drink came first, and a bit of housekeeping second, and then children third.' Reginald, who was evacuated to the village of Weston Green near Bicester in Oxfordshire, came from Bethnal Green where:

> If you came from a large family people would say, 'you lot were sent to Sunday School every week weren't you?' because that would be the only time your mum and dad could get it together. They had be no privacy otherwise. Kids slept in the same room as their mum and dad until quite a late age. There wasn't anywhere else. Then when I got older, I had to sleep on a chair in the kitchen.

As he waited to be 'chosen', Reg noticed:

> A woman starting to look at the evacuees' hair and opening their mouths, but one of the helpers stepped in and pushed her out of the way. 'They might come from

Left: Pupils of Albany Road School, Camberwell, enjoy the delights of the seaside at Weymouth, the south coast town to which they had been evacuated in September 1939.

29

She's in the Ranks too!

CARING FOR EVACUEES IS A NATIONAL SERVICE

ISSUED BY THE MINISTRY OF HEALTH

the East End,' she said, 'but they're human beings. They're children, not animals.'

Many a mother's parting injunction to her children had been: 'You must look after your sister ... you *must* stick together and not be separated,' and this could make it hard to place a family of four of five when many homes were only prepared to take in one or two evacuees. Irene Weller and her brothers had arrived in Stratford-upon-Avon:

not far from Birmingham at all. It probably only took us an hour, maybe less. We were thrilled ... but we soon found it was a snooty town. ... They didn't like interlopers and they certainly didn't want anyone from Birmingham there. We went into this very old school which was the reception centre. There was a coal fire in every room. We were told to sit down, and if there weren't any chairs, we had to sit on the floor. ... Various people kept coming and going and I realised that the number of children was dwindling. And I looked out of the window and it was dusk and we were still there. We'd been there since morning. It must have been about 8 o'clock and we three were the only ones left. Looking back I realise it must have been that no one wanted three children, and who could blame them? I remember the teacher saying to various people, 'They're very well-behaved children, I'm sure they wouldn't be any trouble at all,' and the lady would say, 'Oh, three children. No thank you.'

By this time it was really dark and I was getting frightened and I was beginning to think what's going to happen to us? And my little brother had started to cry and say that he wanted to go home. And eventually one of the teachers came up to us and said, 'Now come along Irene, you and your brothers are going to a really nice place, but you will have to split up from your brothers because that's how it is.' She was very kind really, but my brothers started really to cry then, and I kept remembering what my mother had said: 'Don't let go of them, Irene. All keep together. Don't let them part you.' So my brothers were crying and I was sobbing too, and this billeting officer came and put me in his car – I'd never been in a car before – and he took me to this bungalow. And he knocked on the door and it opened and a great big black dog bounded out and put his paws on my shoulder and a grey-haired lady came to the door and said words I have never forgotten. She said: 'Well, come in. I didn't want you, but come in anyway.' But she was very nice after that. She was well over 60 and she and her husband, who was a train driver and was very kind, had never had children of their own. The woman showed me to my room and it was the first time I'd ever slept in a room of my own. But soon the pillow was wringing wet because I just sobbed and sobbed and cried myself to sleep.

Billeting officers did have legal powers to compel those with surplus accommodation to take in evacuees, but for obvious reasons they were reluctant to use them in the case of children. Some prosecutions were brought, but fines were insignificant and were often overturned on appeal. Persuasion was the best method, but it was not always successful. A letter in the *North Wales Chronicle* recounted such a scene:

30

'Fashion had come to a full stop ... in the mockingly sunny and hot summer' of 1940, wrote Janey Ironside, who was then a would-be clothes designer and went on to be Professor of Fashion Design at the Royal College of Art in the 1950s. So she 'took on voluntary work at a home for those evacuees whose billetors could not cope with the nits, the scabies, the impetigo and bed-wetting that children had brought with them from the slums of Birmingham. I went to the home every afternoon and to amuse them I made drawings of them. They loved Mrs "Iminside's" efforts and there was competition as to who should be the next sitter.'

'Wish me luck as you wave me goodbye ...' A mother takes her leave of her soldier husband as she and her three children evacuate from London in the summer of 1940.

31

A little crowd of homeless schoolboys evacuated from Liverpool sat huddled on the pavement in one of the most well-to-do roads in Bangor, outside the house of a married couple who refused to take them. The billeting officer had argued and begged, 'You have seven empty rooms and no responsibilities,' they pleaded. 'Can't you manage even two of these tired children?' 'No, I cannot,' snapped the woman and closed the door. While the billeting officers discussed what to do with the children the garden gate opened and the 'lady' of the house emerged followed by her husband. They were going to Church! They stepped daintily through the pathetic little bundles, haversacks and gas masks and the children watched them, saying nothing. They passed by on the other side.

If some of the evacuees (or those who accompanied them) were disappointed with the reception they received, many of those waiting to receive them were shocked by the 'urchins' that arrived on their doorsteps. A farmer's wife from Bury was reported to have been horrified when her evacuees arrived from Liverpool in rags 'and the first thing to do was to rig them out. Of course she was not really supposed to do this, but it would have been impossible to wash their clothes.' There were reports of children arriving sewn into brown paper or calico for the winter (who, in normal circumstances, would not be 'unwrapped' until spring). Shoes were found to be entirely inadequate for country mud – indeed Liverpool was christened 'plimsoll city' since this was all the footwear many of its poorest children possessed – and many children were reported neither to own any underwear nor to have ever worn a nightdress or pyjamas. At first there were no grants available to kit out the inadequately equipped, and the sum householders received for taking in an evacuee – 10/6d for one child or 8/6d for each child if there were more

**'There's so much space in the country.'
Evacuees from Blackfriars in London, and
Gravesend in Kent billeted at Dartington
Hall in Devon, return from a walk with
their teacher.**

than one – was hardly adequate to cover the cost of feeding a growing child, and certainly not for buying clothing or boots.

Within a couple of days of arriving in Weymouth, Dorothy Hoyles and her staff were receiving complaints about 'verminous heads'. She was disconcerted to find that the local clinic nurses claimed to be so overwhelmed with nit-infested children that 'the only method used by them was to shave the heads completely as the quickest means of cure'. This was a humiliating experience for confused small children and in effect an assault; Miss Hoyles hastened to procure some soft soap, paraffin, vinegar and special fine-toothed steel combs to distribute to the foster parents so they could deal with the problem in a more humane way. A Lancashire chemist reported that one woman had bought 'a cake of sheep dip to wash the head of a girl she had taken in' and he had sold 'a great many dust combs in my shop this week'.

In Wrexham in Wales, the Medical Officer reported that of the 800 children he had examined on their arrival, ten had the skin condition impetigo; 35 per cent of the girls and 11 per cent of the boys were hosts to head lice; five children were suffering from malnutrition. But horror stories of slum children suffering from the diseases of dirt and neglect were exaggerated. They bespoke the moral indignation many country people felt about the 'townies' who had invaded their rural homes, though the poor condition of some inner-city evacuees often indicated not so much parental neglect as the appalling pre-war housing conditions, with no running water and inadequate lavatory facilities. It also showed the misplaced complacency of urban authorities who had assured the reception areas that they would not be receiving 'verminous and scrofulous children' and had failed to admit that, in the rush to get the children away, it had been impossible for them to undergo any sort of medical examination prior to departure.

Although most children tried movingly hard to fit into their new homes, and foster parents to make them feel welcome, it was again the stories of what was seen as bad behaviour and alien ways that tended to circulate most widely in those early days. Outraged hosts besieged billeting officers with reports of children who were not house-trained, defecated in a corner, urinated against the wall or 'behind the door', refused to take a bath or sleep in a bed since 'that was where the dead are laid out', swore like troopers, declined 'good plain country fare' – greens in particular – and demanded pie and chips with copious quantities of tea (or even beer), tormented animals and younger children, broke windows and the furniture, and generally caused havoc. Then there was the bed-wetting problem, which must have been very trying for hosts but again often spoke less of poor parenting than of the psychological trauma of being torn away from home and familiar surroundings at a young age, often with no real understanding of why and certainly no knowledge of for how long. Some foster parents understood this, and with patience and understanding many evacuees eventually settled down and the bed-wetting ceased. But some hosts were less understanding and punished children harshly for their 'misdemeanours' – beating them, rubbing their noses in the soiled bedding, making small children wash their wet sheets, and even in one case chaining a small Liverpool evacuee outside in a dog kennel for the night. For a few children, enuresis was a long-term problem that would need specialist treatment.

Not all the shocks were one way: some children found themselves living in very primitive conditions since poverty was not confined to the inner cities in Britain of the 1930s. Eleanor Smith was anxious to point out that:

> [Although] we went under the government scheme, [we] came from very respectable homes. Some of the girls ended up in tiny cottages, three to a single bed, with bedbugs which they had never seen in their lives. I wasn't allowed to wash my hair for four months since we had to bring the water up a hill from a village pump.

The government evacuation scheme had been put into effect on Friday 1 September 1939. Soon after 11 a.m. on Sunday 3 September, Irene Weller was:

> sitting in the lounge (only we called it the parlour then) waiting for the Prime Minister [Neville Chamberlain] to give his message. … And I was praying that the war wouldn't start, but of course it did. And the lady looked at me and said, 'Well, you're going to be with me for some time, because as you've just heard the war has started.'

34

Householders who had agreed to take in evacuated schoolchildren were issued with cards to display in their windows as evidence of their involvement in this vital part of National Service. Design by Abram Games.

2 'Not quite the war we had been expecting...'

The Women's Voluntary service (WVS) was set up at the request of the Home Office in June 1938 to recruit women into the ARP (Air Raid Precautions) service. But its brief grew much wider and helping with evacuees was among the most important early war work the WVS undertook. By 1943 membership had risen to close on a million, and it remained at this figure throughout the war.

As the Prime Minister, Neville Chamberlain, was sombrely telling the nation in a radio (or wireless, as it was more usually called in 1939) broadcast at 11.15 on 3 September 1939 that Britain was at war with Germany, 16-year-old Nina Masel was playing the piano in the front room of her family's semi-detached house in Romford in Essex. Suddenly her mother 'burst in shouting "Stop that noise," and flung open the window, letting in the scream of the air raid siren, and the scuffling noise of neighbours in a hurry.' Nina's father took control:

> 'All get your gas masks. … Steady, no panicking! … Every man for himself. … Keep in the passage!' My small sister (11) began to sob: 'Will it be alright?' she kept querying. My mother was frightened, but was trying to take hold of herself. My heart beat hard for a few seconds and then it calmed down. I think my brother and sister felt much the same as I did. We gathered in the passage (we had no shelter) and sat on the stairs. After a few minutes we decided that it was a false alarm or a trial, so we went to the front gate (all except my mother and small sister, who kept calling for us to come back) and remained there until the All Clear was given. A few babies were crying and air-raid wardens with gas masks and helmets were running up and down.

Nina was right: it was a false alarm, the first of many that would come throughout the first year of the war before the Blitz finally started on 7 September 1940 – though there would be frequent raids, mainly on airfields, shipping and other military targets, some resulting in death and injury, before that date.

This period, known as the 'twilight war' or the 'bore war', or later almost universally by a phrase coined in America, the 'phoney war', was a strange, unsettling period, particularly for families as they waited for husbands, brothers, sons to be conscripted to fight in a war that didn't seem to be happening – at least not on the home front. It was very different at sea, and of course in Poland.

These uncertain months proved to be both a severe test of the evacuation programme, and a breathing space to try to get things right. On 12 September 1939 a reassuring story had appeared in the *South London Press*, illustrated with photographs taken by Miss Hoyles of children from her school playing on the sand at Weymouth. The head teacher of Fircroft Road Infants' School in Tooting joined in the cheerful report, pronouncing that 'the people of Littlehampton are the kindest in the world,' and went on to report that her school's evacuation from Balham station the previous week had gone very smoothly and that 'there were very few tears and in nearly every instance the children were happily

Evacuees dutifully carry their gas masks as they paddle in a stream in Buckinghamshire on 6 September 1939.

36

placed. The few exceptions were noted and no pains will be spared to get everyone comfortable.' Indeed from day one, Dorothy Hoyles and her staff had been 'very busy all day far into the night … investigating complaints' from the children about their billets and from the hosts about the evacuees they had been sent. She called a meeting on the beach at Weymouth and talked to the children about the importance of cleanliness, early bedtimes, trying to be helpful and remembering to write home to their parents, and made arrangements to have similar meetings with her pupils every day. Then Miss Hoyles had to rush off to sort out the case of one of her small charges who was threatened with being moved from his billet for throwing one of his host's child's toys into the sea, and also to find a new billet for a little boy who 'had given dissatisfaction by bed-wetting'. She was fortunate to find 'another foster father who agreed to give him a trial as he would like to tackle a difficult case'.

Golden day followed golden day in that beautiful Indian summer when the world was at war again, as Miss Hoyles and her colleagues (and teachers like them all over Britain) rushed around 'visiting misfits', including one boy who 'is extremely unhappy and arrangements will have to be made to move him. His foster mother cannot comfort him. He evidently needs another influence.'

The staff 'visited homes where children needed more clothing' and arranged for the distribution of clothing that had been donated, 'dealt with "heads" in the playground', took the children on excursions into the countryside and organised games and picnics on the beach. It was fortunate that the weather was so perfect, since school didn't start for the evacuees until 18 September at the earliest and the children had to be kept occupied, both to keep them out from under the feet of their foster parents (or host families as some

preferred to be called) and also to try to take their minds off how much they might be missing home – mum in particular.

Meanwhile Dr Brock and her staff spent *their* days 'covering 40 to 50 miles a day' of the Kent countryside:

> meeting groups of staff and girls [from Mary Datchelor School] on village greens, dealing with billeting problems, and generally keeping in touch with our scattered flock, helped by bright sunshine and abundance of petrol [still]; and at last our numbers came right when the last four children were run to earth at 'Faraway Farm'. After about ten days of seeing people, telephoning, writing and talking, we managed to move about 250 girls into Ashford. We left staff and girls in the more accessible villages. ... [These] villages gave our boys and girls a warm welcome, and they were soon taking part in the life of their village, helping in their homes and on the farms, singing in the church choir, playing games, walking, cycling and helping to man Air Raid Wardens' posts. Many girls cycled into Ashford, and some came by bus, and others, in spite of being Londoners, learnt to walk.

East Ender Reginald Baker had been billeted with the village blacksmith and his wife in a village near Bicester, and was very impressed that the family had a tablecloth on the table for *every meal* rather than the sheet of newspaper he was used to at home:

> 'Granny' Dorling bought me a pair of Wellington boots because my own shoes had holes in with bits of cardboard stuffed in to keep out the wet – only it didn't. It

Above: A series of photographs issued by the Ministry of Information to show how successful the official government evacuation scheme could be.

37

In the first of the series (left) **Mrs Carter is seen setting off from Victoria station in London to visit her children in the country.**

Next (centre)**, Michael and Angela Carter run to greet their mother on her arrival at their farmhouse billet.**

Mission accomplished (right)**. Mrs Carter, apparently satisfied with her children's wartime home, returns to London. Michael and Angela – looking somewhat downcast – go with their foster mother to wave her off.**

A painting by Ethel Hatch of 'Evacuees in Oxford in 1942.' Not all those who sought sanctuary in the city of dreaming spires when the bombs began to fall on London were so fortunate. Hundreds of East Enders were put up in the Majestic Cinema, many forced to sleep between the tip-up seats, in the aisles or in the orchestra pit.

38

was very nice of her because she didn't get much money for us – me and another boy. … We'd climb trees and I cut a branch from one of the trees and I'd use it to jump over streams and things, and we'd paddle in the streams and collect frogspawn – there was just so much space in the country.

When Irene Weller and her bothers arrived in Stratford-upon-Avon:

It was the apple season … and a lot of householders had surplus apples, so they'd put them in a box outside the gate with a notice saying 'Please Take One.' We couldn't believe it. We had only seen apples in shop windows before; we had no idea they came off trees.

Peter Holloway was just four years old when he was evacuated with his ten-year-old brother from a 'terraced house near Millwall football ground' in east London.

Angmering on Sea in Sussex proved to be our destination and it was as different from Bermondsey as could be imagined. I could only remember row upon row of back-to-back soot-blackened terraced houses surrounded by factories and a network of railways leading to and from Dockland. In contrast, the village of Angmering was a neat cluster of pink-bricked houses with a row of attractive shops set in a sea of green lawns and stately trees.

Boys of Malvern College which was evacuated to Blenheim Palace, Churchill's birthplace and ancestral home, study beneath a priceless Flemish tapestry depicting the Duke of Marlborough in battle. The palace's Great Hall was used as the school dining room, while the Long Library and staterooms served as dormitories for the boys.

Peter and his brother and three other children were claimed by:

> a very pretty young woman dressed in a sky-blue frock and with short cropped hair. … She signed a certificate of some sort and led five of us away to a wonderful new motor car. I'm certain none of us had travelled in a car before and there was a great sense of excitement as we clambered in. … Miss Grant … turned the car into a long straight road, at the end of which was a pebbly beach and my first sight of the sea … No one ever forgets their first sight of the sea, water and sky that seems to go on for ever. … Half a mile away was our new home. It was an enormous private estate called 'The Thatches', complete with garaging for seven motor cars, stables for horses and a private beach below the extensive gardens. … We were taken through a large open door … into the hall … where a maid in a black and white uniform appeared and led us upstairs. … My brother and I were put into a huge bath where the maid proceeded to scrub off the grime of Bermondsey. … It proved to be a house of many bathrooms, bedrooms, small and large spaces. We hardly needed to be told that the owners must be enormously rich. … During the following weeks we grew accustomed to the grandiose style of living which was routine for the Grant family. Sometimes they joined us for the evening meal, but usually it was presided over by the butler and servants.

Stanley and two of the girls, Patsy and Mary, went to school in Angmering, while Peter and another little girl, Pauline:

'*The war will be won on the playing fields of England.' Girls from Harrogate College who had been evacuated to Lord Swinton's country house at Masham, Yorkshire, playing hockey in the grounds.*

40

went to a nursery for mornings only nearby. We were taken by car and picked up again when school was over. In no time at all, we became used to the lavish attention heaped upon us and the good food and clothing which came our way. Patsy and Stanley were learning to ride horses after school along the broad expanse of sand that appeared at low tide … and had formed a close relationship, after a difficult beginning, and we all knew they had been 'experimenting' when left alone in the big house. … The 'Phoney War' continued, or at least no sound of trouble reached our well-protected ears at The Thatches. The neighbouring houses were owned by famous people of stage, screen and radio, or so my brother said and he knew about these things. … Stanley was fast becoming a competent horseman and we were all growing accustomed to our extravagant lifestyle. …

We were rapidly growing away from our parents and all of this must have been obvious to them on their fleeting visits to Angmering. … Stanley had been doing well at school and the Grants had realised quite early on that he had a restlessly enquiring mind. They had taken to him in a rather special way and tried to foster his obvious natural intelligence. It was this, as much as anything else, that my parents were concerned about and feared that they were somehow losing him [and decided to bring us] back to the smog and grime of London … the school where the only play area was the tarmacadam roof of the building and the only sight of green – the paintwork around the school. … Our Life of Riley was over. … We had had spent rather less than a year in Angmering but the effect was out of all proportion to the time which had passed.

Hazel Brown had it pretty grand at her first billet too. She and her two friends from Mary Datchelor School in Camberwell were taken:

by car to a lovely country house in huge grounds. … Next morning we found we were in the home of Sir Jack and Lady Pym and their four children. Lady Pym came into the kitchen and told us the house rules. We were confined to the servants' quarters indoors, to use only the back stairs, and outside to keep to the side gardens. The servants were an Austrian couple, refugees, as cook and butler. They spoke little English and obviously disliked having to do the extra work that we entailed. And there was Dorothy the kitchen maid, just left the village school and more than ready to be friendly, but of course she had work to do.

This privileged – if unwelcoming – life came to an end when the girls were moved nearer to their school in Ashford, and Hazel Brown's next billet could not have been more of a contrast:

Right: Children from Albany Road School, Camberwell, do handstands at a holiday club arranged to keep them occupied during out of school hours in Weymouth.

Mr and Mrs Holmes were young with no family of their own. They asked me to call them Mr and Mrs because they felt too young to be known as auntie and uncle, as became the custom. I had a little bedroom at the back of the house. He worked in the local wood yards and was not called up because it was a reserved occupation [necessary

41

Albany Rd School Unit: Holiday Club: Aerobatic Turns.

42

An education interrupted. Evacuees from Woodmansterne Road School in Streatham, south London, use the village hall in Farmers, Carmarthen, as a classroom where their teachers attempt to teach classes of different ages different subjects but in very close proximity.

work for the prosecution of the war], and she stayed at home – at that time not many married women went out to work. They were very kind and made me welcome. … The big drawback was no bathroom. I'd read about homes like this but had never experienced one. The toilet was outside and the kitchen had just a cold water tap. In the corner was an old-fashioned boiler which had to be filled with buckets from the sink and a fire kindled underneath. This happened every Monday morning for washday and every Saturday night for baths. The tin bath hung on a nail outside and was brought in and put on the kitchen floor. In winter it was really cosy, but such hard work. As I was the youngest, I had the first bath, then the adults. Mrs Holmes's younger sister lived there too; she worked in the Co-op and cycled to work.

Rosemary Mines's billet was on the grand side. Aged five, she had been evacuated with her Australian-born mother and younger sister from south-east London to a large house in Caterham in Surrey:

What the wealthy owners felt about being invaded by evacuees from the city, I do

not know although they really seemed friendly, and did not keep aloof from us at all but seeming rather to welcome our company. ... There were several other families sharing the downstairs with us. Other children, the excitement of a new baby and an older couple. The perfect extended family. Each family unit was based in one room but we often dined communally at the large kitchen table. I remember thoroughly enjoying eating with so many people even though the fare was baked beans or other wartime food. I recall no dispute whatsoever – we all got along beautifully and in retrospect it seems a happy time, although we were in fact to be right in the flight path of the Battle of Britain planes and heard them passing overhead many nights. ...

What to do about our schooling was rather a problem. The nearest school was several miles away. The daughter of the family who owned the house tried to teach us, without too much success. Firmly embedded in my mind were early knitting lessons – from somewhere thick wool and needles were purchased and small tea cosies knitted in garter stitch. I suppose the main education was in the country walks, the playing with other children, the communal living, visits from our father

'Wherever there is space.' Children from Brockley Central School in south London had their lessons in the converted saloon bar of The Old Star public house in Lingfield, Surrey.

" You—you—ex-evacuees ! ! "

Above: Punch, 17 January 1940.

Below: Evacuees have an open-air lesson as a farmer ploughs his field. In the first weeks of autumn 1939 when the weather was good, and no suitable accommodation was ready, classrooms might be set up in the fields or on village greens.

44

who was in the fire service and helped put out fires while London burned, even our grandparents who came down to visit. … I think we did all go to school one day, but it was rather far away and on the way back we saw [a parachutist] landing so the mission was abandoned and we never went again.

Schooling was an acute problem in the autumn of 1939, and the education of many children continued to suffer throughout the war. An official report on London published in 1943 concluded that:

> The shock of the war and evacuation has been heavy on London schools. … Schools were broken up and rapidly lost their identity. Reorganisation and even merging with local schools have been continuous; changes of staff and re-evacuations have made the continuity of work and even syllabuses practically impossible.

The situation was much the same over most of the country.

Teacher Stanley Reed had been evacuated with his class of West Ham children to a village in Berkshire:

> A muddy path led past the churchyard to a brick Gothic schoolhouse, with narrow pointed windows and an immensely high pitched roof. There was a tiny dirt yard, divided by a fence into Boys and Girls, with rudimentary lavatories. The school had no water supply and every morning the bigger boys fetched buckets of water from the horse-trough outside the church. Inside were two rooms, the Big Room for seven to fourteens and the Baby Room for fives to sevens. The furniture was ancient and scarred, the paint dark brown. Each room had a tortoise stove, the heat from which rose straight up into the vast roof and fluttered the cobwebs. The one concession to progress was gas lighting, comprising rickety brackets suspended on immensely long pipes from the roof. …
>
> The village schoolmistress, plump and pleasant Miss Dickie, was young and efficient. … The Baby Room was in the charge of an elderly lady of the kind one could imagine in charge of a Dame's School a century earlier.
>
> The school had a roll call of 19; somehow nearly 30 East Enders had to be absorbed. 'We decided to merge the

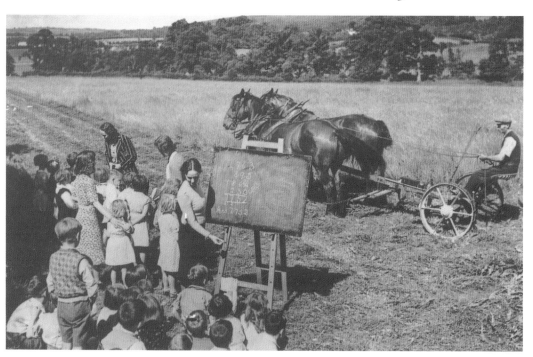

London and village children, age-grouping them into three,' with Mr Reed teaching the top group.

> We also merged such specialist talent as we commanded, I teaching Art throughout the School, though sadly handicapped by having only ruled exercise book paper and too few pencils to go round, and Miss Dickie taking the Music. She and I shared the Big Room, with no more division between our classes than a few extra inches between her rows of desks and mine. Materials presented the main problem; for weeks the children had to share pens, taking it in turn to write when there was anything to write on.

June Fidler, who had been evacuated from Peckham, recalls that in her village school:

> The exercise books were cut in half with a guillotine or whatever and we had a half one each; they did the same with pencils. We normally had to write with a dip pen, using ink which a class monitor mixed up from powder. It was horrible stuff, but it ran out so we had to do all our writing with our half-pencils. And the textbooks, what there were of those, we had to share.

Betty Helliar found that there was no purpose-built school in the village of Peters Green near Luton to accommodate her infants' class from north London:

> The school was housed in the church, the juniors in the nave and the infants in the vestry. … At the first opportunity I called at the school and made myself known to Miss Stevens [the headmistress] and any hopes of our joining the school were dashed when I saw they were full up. I also noted they were short of stock. … I had no idea what to do. … Ought I to try and make some arrangements for school myself or would that be presuming? After all I was only a very junior member of staff. On the other hand something must be done and I was the only one there to do it. The foster parents could not be expected to look after the evacuees all day when their own children were at school, and I certainly didn't want my little Londoners to be a nuisance or get into mischief, so I decided we would have to have an open air school in the nearest stubble field and keep

'We'll Keep a Welcome in the Valleys'. London children evacuated to Wales are taught 'some necessary Welsh words.' Welsh was extensively spoken in home, school and chapel in many parts of North Wales in 1939, and in some rural areas, almost half the population could only speak Welsh.

45

46

Above: 'Gas Mask Drill' drawing of schoolboys by Alexander Macpherson, 1941.

school hours until better arrangements could be made. Fortunately the weather was fine and dry for about three weeks. We had oral lessons, poetry, singing, drama, nature study, and we went for long walks (always with our gas masks). ... The children enjoyed the novelty of the open air school [and] were constantly learning even if the curriculum was unconventional.

Eventually the vicar, 'who understood my predicament about a roof over our heads ... said it would be possible to use the village hall once arrangements were made about heating and cleaning.' Betty Helliar and another teacher arranged to take a car back to Stoke Newington one weekend:

to raid our old school for some stock. ... We raided our respective classroom cupboards, taking quantities of exercise books, reading books, pencils, crayons, drawing paper and my percussion band. We each gave the school keeper a letter confirming we took full responsibility for removing the stock for the use of LCC pupils. The following week we would be able to have use of the village hall with a piano, chairs, two coke stoves (one of which smoked) and a small kitchen and WCs, so the LCC school at Peters Green became a reality. Each day we went to the church school for assembly, then we marched down the road to the village hall to begin lessons.

As was the pattern in many evacuated schools, Miss Hoyles arranged a 'double shift' system for educating the Albany Road children while they were in Weymouth. From 18 September 1939 when the school reopened, some classes were taught from 9 a.m. to 12.30 p.m. and the others from 1 p.m. to 4.30 p.m. In the fine weather assemblies were held in the playground. But the problem of suitable premises continued to create a tiresome situation, and as the weather grew more inclement throughout the autumn, Dorothy Hoyles was regularly obliged to record in her School Log: 'Assembly and religious instruction in Church. All classes dispersed for walks and excursions [frequently] in spite of the fog and fine drizzle that was falling.'

The military had already requisitioned the most suitable parish hall for its purposes, 'leaving our infants with no assembly room or place for activities', and the vicar seems to have been singularly unhelpful about the evacuees' educational needs. Eventually a local Methodist church agreed to reduce the rent for its church hall to be used by some classes, while others occupied premises nearby once they had been cleaned up, the walls distempered and the broken windows repaired.

Miss Hoyles was concerned about the lack of shelters too: at the end of September she had her:

first practice of using the trenches provided in the adjoining field for the use of

The antithesis of 'Happy Families'? A wartime children's card game showing a disparate variety of evacuees, their teachers and householders on whom the children were billeted.

Left: Winifred Beer in her school uniform in September 1939 and with fellow pupils of her Portsmouth School that was evacuated to Salisbury in Wiltshire.

London children, who had remained in the capital, being taught at Greek Road School in south-east London, presumably during a gas-mask practice, and possibly in an air-raid shelter.

children during air raids. The youngest infants were provided with concrete dugouts, and the older children with open zig-zag trenches three-and-a-half feet deep [if trenches were straight, a blast could pass directly along them, felling the occupants like ninepins]. The trenches are dug in clay and do not seem adequate protection in their present condition as a portion of the taller children's heads still showed above the ground. Moreover the teachers were considerably more exposed by reason of their greater height.

As negotiations were proceeding in late September, the doughty headmistress replied to a National Union of Teachers' representative who was travelling round the country visiting evacuated schools, that while she was:

Writing home

During the Second World War letters were an essential form of communication. Long-distance telephone calls were expensive and unreliable, and the Post Office instructed 'Please Telephone Less,' explaining: 'Social chatter over the telephone networks may hold up vitally important war talks.'

So letters became an essential link between wives parted from husbands, parents from children. Evacuees eagerly waited for the post, and were desperately disappointed not to get a letter when others did. Most wrote home regularly. A moving indication of how long the war lasted is the way in which an evacuee's childish scrawl on the outbreak of war had become neat, joined-up writing with complete, punctuated sentences by 1945.

Evacuees' letters – many illustrated with sketches – painted a picture of busy lives, interspersed with requests for new clothes to replace those outgrown or outworn, pocket money, 'gloves so I can throw snowballs', a favourite doll or a stamp collection 'so I can have swops' to be sent.

But too often the letters masked the loneliness the child was feeling, how much she or he was missing home. Sometimes this was because children did not want to upset their parents. At other times the reason was more sinister. The headmistress of a London school evacuated to Wales felt 'very strongly' that her pupils 'should be free to write to their mothers whatever was in their hearts. To put down in black and

27 Arthur Street
Withernsea.
18/2/40

Dear Mummy, I am writing to
ask if you could possibly
knit me a pair of gloves so I
lost one and the other is full
of holes with snowballing. I am
ever so well and have not
had a bilious attack for two
weeks, in fact I am full of
beans.
Hope you are all well
Heaps of love
from Roy

P.S. I have not been
hit by a bomb yet.

PPS I have not been
gassed yet

P.P.SS
I have not
come in
contact
with an air gun yet

Dear Mam and Dad,
I hope
you are keeping well as we
are at present. I received
your letter on Tuesday and I
am thankful you got home
alright. Kenneth was still
crying a long time after
you had gone but the
rabbit had come back to
find its mate so I caught
hold of it and put it
back in the hutch. I think
this is all,
Love from
Gordon

*Above: A letter sent by Roy Child to his
parents in Hull from his evacuation
billet.*

*Above right: A drawing by Dorothy King
in a letter sent home to her parents in
Abbey Wood, south London, from
Maidstone.*

*white what they really felt, when they
were overwhelmed by a patch of
homesickness and misery,' but she
found that 'one custom which wrecked
a number of billets was the practice of
[foster mothers] reading letters – either
from home to the child, or letters which
she had written to her mother or father.
… Once a letter home, containing some
wounding sentence, had been read by a
foster mother, it was very hard to
redeem the situation.'*

29 Cromwell Rd.,
Wednesday.
Dear Mum and Dad,
Thanks very much for the P.O. and
also the cycle spare parts and woodwork apron.
You wrote and said there was a duster as well,
but I couldn't find it, mum. The front piece of
leather on my bike has worn come right off and iron
pieces are sticking out. I can hardly ride my bike
in the wind we have here. I don't know for certain
how much holiday we are having for Christmas,
but there is a rumour going round that we are
having a week. I will let you know when I know
for certain. I haven't heard from Val for weeks but
I suppose 'no news is good news' (ahem! ahem!) You made
my mouth water at the end of your letter, with the
picture of the Christmas pud. On Monday I went
to the pictures to see Robert Donat in 'Goodbye Mr.
Chips.' It is about the life of a schoolmaster, and
is supposed to be one of the best pictures of the year.
I am getting a lot more books from school now.
(algebra, geometry) I still have books from the

very. I have been trying to think out a Christmas
...nt for Mrs. Minter, and have come to the
...usion (?) that she would like a Calender.
...will soon be practising our Christmas carols now,
I suppose, so Roll on Christmas!
Well, thats all for now so
...ood bye to you all from KEN.
Don't forget our 'phone number in case you want
...have a little chat. Canterbury 3641. So-long.

*Above: Ken Gosling reminds his father in
Chatham of his 'phone number in
Canterbury.*

*Above: Gordon Muers's letter home from
his evacuation address in Northallerton,
Yorkshire, to his parents in Sunderland
giving news of his older brother Ken.*

Right: Home-made farmyard toys fashioned by a member of the Women's Land Army for her younger brother.

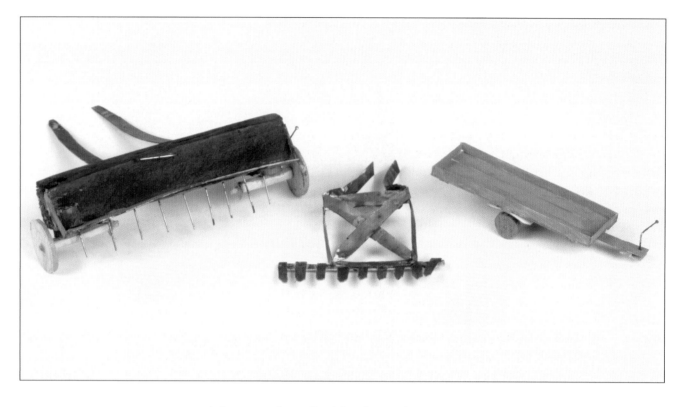

50

CHILDREN are safer in the country ... leave them there

certainly not … 'heartily sick of everything connected to evacuation' … indeed the whole business was very interesting, even absorbing … matters were in such a state of flux that it was necessary to live from day to day – even from hour to hour – in order to keep going.

The situation was not much easier for the intrepid Dr Brock. Having finally managed to locate her Mary Datchelor School pupils in their new abodes, and move many of them:

on September 20th, the actual day on which we had planned to re-open in Camberwell [had war and thus evacuation not intervened] we began to work a double shift with the County School, Ashford girls working from 8.30 to 12.30 and Datchelor girls from 1.0 till 5.0; and we all worked a six-day week. On the same day the Junior School opened at Hothfield in a room in the Village School. But our difficulties were still many. Kent had not begun to build trenches [as protection from air raids] and we were therefore instructed not to have more than 60 girls in the County School at a time. … This limitation of numbers meant that everyone could have one hour's teaching a day. Sixth form groups met at private houses.

Eventually some accommodation was found in a local private school for two of the top classes for two hours a week. 'Girls had to learn to work by themselves and do three hours' homework for one hour's lesson. We all had not only to practise adaptability and resource and independence, but also acquire a new technique of teaching,' concluded the headmistress with masterly understatement.

Things did improve slowly, and by the end of November, the girls were being taught for two hours a day and meetings of the 'Guides, the Dramatic Society, the Orchestra and Choirs, and also some gymnastics and games' had been able to resume in borrowed premises, while a helpful local headmistress allowed the use of her school's laboratories on occasions 'for practical work in Science'.

If schooling was inadequate for the evacuees, however, it was almost non-existent for those children left behind in the cities. Parents had been warned that if they did not send their children out of London on the government's official evacuation scheme, there would be no education provided for them. This was indeed the case for hundreds and thousands who were left with no school, school meals or health services. School buildings in the evacuation areas had been requisitioned wholesale for military or civil defence purposes such as first-aid posts, ARP or AFS (Auxiliary Fire Service) headquarters, gas decontamination centres and even temporary mortuaries, since it was presumed that the children would have all left for the country. Most teachers had gone with schools that had been evacuated, and there was a growing shortage of teachers anyway as men were called up into the forces and a number of younger women opted for war work. Schools were increasingly staffed with older teachers (some brought out of retirement) and married women, and classes grew larger as well as less well equipped. By April 1940 it was estimated that only about half the elementary school children in the danger zones in England and Wales were receiving full-time schooling, around 30 per cent were going to school half time, 10 per cent were being taught at home, and 10 per cent – some 115,000 children – had no schooling at all. Secondary school children fared better, with an estimated 87 per cent of children in full-time schooling, 8 per cent in school half time, but 5 per cent not in school at all. In Scotland some 60 per cent of children in local authority schools were receiving full-time education, 36 per cent half time, and 4 per cent none at all.

51

Above: The charms of the countryside. The rural life was regarded as being redemptive for the many urban 'urchins' who had been evacuated there. In the country such children would lose their wily city ways, and settle down to a slower, more 'natural' life – or so it was hoped by the authorities. 'A cartload of young evacuees ... looking the picture of health' on a farm in Somerset exemplify this perception.

In readiness for Christmas 1940, older schoolgirls evacuees in the Lake District help to fatten geese on a farm at the foot of Langdale Pike.

William Alexander, the newly-appointed education officer for Sheffield, recalled:

I knew I had 55,000 children and no schools open. Then I heard an announcer say 'This is the BBC Home Service.' Home Service – that was the answer. We appealed for 5,000 school rooms in private houses, for which we paid 2/6d a week, and we moved the desks and the furniture from schools into these houses. The children were divided into groups of 12 and each group was taught for an hour and a half a day. Sheffield was, I think, the first place to institute home tuition and many of the children went on receiving it for months, often in people's bedrooms or kitchens. They spent another one and a half hours a day in the local library.

But not all children were so fortunate. Predictably, many of those who had no schooling provided and had nothing to do but hang around the streets all day – 'dead end kids' the journalist Ritchie Calder dubbed them – got into trouble. Hooliganism, vandalism and petty crime increased: in Glasgow twice as many children under 14 were found guilty of theft or housebreaking in 1940 than in the immediate pre-war years.

The situation was a conundrum for the government: some of these unfortunate children – 'starved of education, numbed through lack of direction, and neglected in health', as Ritchie Calder charged – had never left London and other provincial cities, and their numbers were swelling daily with evacuees returning home, which was just what the government did not want to happen. If permission was given for schools to reopen in the danger zones, it would look as if the policy of dispersing children was being abandoned and a return to the cities was condoned.

The largest number of returnees, however, were not schoolchildren but mothers who had been evacuated with their babies and small children. This had been the least successful part of the evacuation scheme. Country people were generally less willing to share their homes – and particularly their kitchens – with another woman than they were to take in unaccompanied children. There were numerous complaints from the hosts about the manners and habits of the adult evacuees: they were accused of being feckless, lazy and dirty, of frequenting pubs, neglecting their children and failing to discipline them properly. For their part, the mothers were unhappy about the lack of welcome they felt was extended to them, and the often stringent rules and regulations householders insisted on. They found the country interminably dull; no wonder they went to the pub. Where else was there to go? No Woolworths, no cinema and maybe a bus into the nearest town once a day if they were lucky. Many missed their husbands and their homes, their friends and neighbours and the shops selling food they were accustomed to, and had no desire

to learn how to make suet puddings, eat home-grown swedes and turnips, or cook cuts of meat they had never previously encountered. By December 1939 nearly 90 per cent of those mothers evacuated in September had returned home.

An important reason for the drift back of schoolchildren as well of mothers and infants was that it became increasingly unclear what they had been evacuated from. No bombs rained down on city homes, no poison gas drifted through city streets. The war that had been expected had not materialised, so many parents who had been reluctant to send their children away in the first place began to bring them home. Sometimes this was because the parents missed their children too much or needed their help. Sometimes it was because parents were concerned that an enforced separation would loosen family ties and that their children would grow away from them and acquire different values, as Peter Holloway's parents had feared.

Sometimes it was the children themselves who were homesick and unhappy. Ronald McGill remembers when he was evacuated at the age of nine with his seven-year-old sister Jean to near Reading:

> There was nothing to do except go to bed and read comics and sob. … 'Dear Mum, we want to come home.' That's what we wrote at the bottom of every letter, and after seven weeks they came down and took us back.

Two-year-olds get acquainted with some cows at 'Toddler's Town', a residential nursery for some 500 children aged between 15 months and five years. Described as 'by far the largest concentration camp of evacuated children', it was situated on a large estate 'somewhere in the Home Counties'.

Occasionally, though, it was suspected that foster mothers reported that the children were unhappy so that the children might be taken home or moved to another billet, and the foster parents would be relieved of their responsibilities.

While probably most children were homesick, missed parents, friends, pets, their toys and familiar surroundings, and longed for the time they could go home again, the distress of some children was more profound. When seven-year-old Dennis Hayes and his brother were evacuated from Portsmouth to Sway in the New Forest, they arrived at their billet:

> as if we were intruders into their family life. And as if it was our fault. … I can remember my brother, who was five, crying most of the night and so the father tied him to a banister at the bottom of the stairs with a long woollen scarf to try to stop him crying, and of course that made him cry even worse.

Gwendoline Watts, who was evacuated from Birmingham to Ashby de la Zouch in Leicestershire, hated it:

> I was treated like a skivvy. I was made to take charge of the child [in her billet], get her up, give her breakfast, look after her when the parents went out. I was falling behind with my school lessons because I wasn't allowed to do any homework before I had put the child to bed, and then I had to turn the light out by 9 o'clock. I had to rush home from school at lunchtime and start preparing the meal and then I had to do all the washing up. … But I didn't write to tell my mother because I knew it would upset her. She used to send me a shilling every week wrapped up in a piece of paper with a letter. … And I saved up all these shillings and one day I went to the bus station and asked the Midlands Red Bus man, 'How much is it to Birmingham?' And he told me and I realised that I had just enough, so I just hopped on the bus and sat in a corner as low down as I could so that I wouldn't be seen because the other girls were going to school at that time. I didn't have anything with me. I'd left everything at the foster parents' house. It was a spur of the moment thing. My mother and father didn't know I was coming. I didn't know what sort of reception I would get but I knew I had to get away from there.
>
> I walked three miles from the bus station and when I got home I didn't have a key so I knocked at the door and my mother came to the door and she said 'What are you doing here?' When I told her why I'd come home, she said 'You should … have written and told me about it and I would have come down and sorted it out.' The school had been closed down in Birmingham but eventually I was able to get myself a job as a telephone receptionist in a Birmingham factory that was making parts for submarines.

Farrance Street School, Limehouse, was evacuated to Somerton in Somerset on 1 September 1939. Mary Mudd (now Mrs Speaight), the young art mistress, 'put the pupils' desks back to back and spread out huge sheets of sugar paper so the children – most of whom had never seen the country before – could paint pictures of their new rural life. They did linocuts, too. They were all so vivid, the children really loved the countryside, and all there was to see.'

Royal duties (junior branch)

The future Queen Elizabeth II was 13 in September 1939. With her sister Princess Margaret Rose she spent most of the war at Windsor, where during the Blitz the princesses took shelter in the dungeons deep beneath the Castle.

The royal children as lived normal a life as possible there, with their usual tutoring, riding in Windsor Great Park and Girl Guide activities. But they too had wartime responsibilities. Each Christmas the two princesses took part in a Christmas pantomime, performed for the staff to raise money for one of the Queen's wartime charities.

In October 1940 Princess Elizabeth made a five-minute broadcast to 'the children of the Empire' during Children's Hour on the BBC. It suggested that the royal children also knew what it was like to be separated from their parents in wartime, though in fact the King and Queen spent most nights at Windsor with the girls, and even Churchill's private secretary found himself embarrassed by 'the sloppy sentiment [the princess] was made to express'.

'My sister is by my side,' Princess Elizabeth concluded her talk, 'and we are both going to say goodnight to you. Come on Margaret.' 'Goodnight, and good luck to you all,' piped up her 10-year-old sister.

Princess Elizabeth (right) and Princess Margaret watching a march past of the Canadian Forestry Corps at Balmoral in September 1941.

55

Irene Weller would:

> never go anywhere without my brothers. If I was invited anywhere, I'd say, 'I've got to bring my brothers too.' And in the evening I had to be in before dusk, and my little brother [who was billeted in a house across the road] would cling onto me, and there were always tears in his eyes – every night. I know evacuation didn't affect some children. But it did him. Very much.

Dorothy King recalls that:

> I wrote home regularly. The letters sounded chirpy enough, but I know that sometimes I sat over them crying alone in the dining room. I was too old to be sent to bed with Hilary and Vivien [her host's two young daughters] and too young to share the parents' evening. Used to a lot of attention from a protective mother,

Right: Various experiments were tried to make the evacuation experience work – for children, foster parents and teachers. One scheme was a communal feeding centre run by volunteers, at Chipping Campden in the Cotswolds, where evacuees, 'mostly from the East End of London' could have a meal daily for 3d a head. The meal was hot, but judging by the children's headgear in December 1940, the premises were not.

Opposite

Above: Anxious that the children from her Camberwell school should enjoy their first Christmas as evacuees in Weymouth, their headmistress, Miss Hoyles, arranged a full programme of activities for them.

Below: A further example of the government campaign urging mothers not to bring their children back to the cities. In this example, an ethereal Hitler whispers seductively in an uncertain mother's ear.

I was now, I felt, only a peripheral part of a strange family! I was often miserable.

Although Dorothy never asked to come home, her letters were often wistful. 'Everybody's parents seemed to be down here to visit their children,' she wrote, 'despite what Miss Summers [the headmistress] said, and Miss Summers was quoting from a newspaper.'

'Dear Mummy, please remember this address as it takes up a lot of room,' wrote Kathleen Crawley in every letter home from her billet in a village near Ashford in Kent, though her mother, perhaps rather tactlessly, often headed *her* letters simply 'Home Sweet Home'.

'Don't forget our 'phone number in case you want to have a little chat. Canterbury 3691. So long,' Ken Gosling hopefully appended as a postscript to every letter he wrote home to his parents in Chatham, sometimes even suggesting that his father 'need not waste a penny ha'penny stamp, but could ring instead.'

If their child was evacuated to somewhere not far from home, parents could visit them in their billets. For parents whose children had been despatched to the other end of the country, however, such visits were rare – or even out of the question. On the outbreak of war the railway companies had abolished cheap day-return tickets, and it was not until November 1939 that some concessionary fares were introduced. Cheap day tickets could be bought for Sunday travel to a limited number of destinations. But the cost for poor Liverpool families, for example, to travel to the very tip of North Wales to visit their evacuated children was invariably prohibitive.

Grenville Atherton who had been evacuated all of 20 miles from Manchester to Macclesfield in September became, along with many of his classmates, 'part-time evacuees' in the winter of 1939–40, with 'hordes of red and black uniforms' leaving by train or bus after Saturday morning school and returning first thing on Tuesday. Many schools, however, discouraged too many parental visits, and particularly weekend visits home, since these were deemed to unsettle the children and make it harder to adjust to their new ways of life. Irene Weller's mother and older sister came to visit her and her brothers after they had been away for a month:

> It was traumatic and though I had wanted them to come so much, it was dreadful when it was time for them to go. Terrible. I had to tear my brothers away. It was awful and my Mother said, 'I shall never come again.' Apparently when they got home, one of my sisters said, 'Oh fetch them back. It's not right.'

One of the first letters Dr Brock sent to the parents of Mary Datchelor pupils addressed this point:

> We are trying to keep life normal and healthy and happy for your children. … We cannot reproduce home conditions or guarantee freedom from all discomforts or difficulties. … This is a war; and much that was possible in Camberwell is impossible in the conditions that face us here. We have to distinguish between

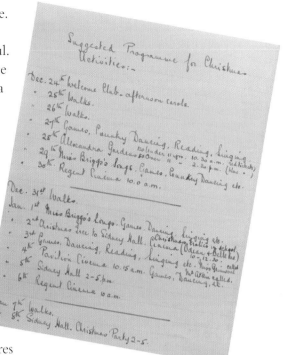

grumbles and real difficulties, and it is interesting to see how differently girls react to this test of experience in the spirit of adventure, and with that sense of proportion which, instead of magnifying difficulties distinguishes between those which must be expected as inevitable, and those for which some other solution must be found. You will help both your daughters and the Staff if you will encourage your daughters to meet this experience in the spirit of adventure.

The pupils' planned visit home at half-term in October had to be cancelled, apparently because of restrictions on travel, but the real blow fell at Christmas 1939. At the end of November, Dr Brock:

> had to tell the School that the Authorities had decided not to give leave of absence during the period 23rd–31st December, their purpose being not only to prevent children from returning to evacuated areas, but also to leave the railways and roads free, particularly for troops returning on leave; for Kent was of course a highway from the coast to London.

Despite their disappointment the girls (and staff):

> rose magnificently to the occasion and greeted our plans for keeping Christmas as a School family with hilarious zest. … A Christmas gift of a cheque from the Clothworkers' Company … made many delightful extras possible for us, from turkeys, home-grown by a foster father, to buses to take the girls back to the villages after parties. … Heavy snowfalls added to the fun of the holidays, though they complicated transport; and the countryside looked enchanting.

But it couldn't be a proper Christmas – either for children or parents.

Christmas was, as the government feared, the most vulnerable time for their evacuation programme: parents wanted their children home, and children wanted to be there, and once home, they might not return.

Miss Hoyles had been fighting a battle all autumn to keep her pupils in Weymouth By the end of September, nine children had already 'returned to London despite remonstrances to the contrary'. On 10 October: 'Visit of Rose Blackburn's sister and fiancé to ask for Rose's return to London: Cause: 14 years of age and suitable employment.' Miss Hoyles and a colleague 'tried lengthy persuasion … but to no avail. Elder sister said that Rose's earnings were needed to pay government's recovery of expenses for younger children.' Five days later: 'Visit from Joan Derby's sister who wished to remove her. (Reason given: Joan was fretting). Would not be persuaded. Visited Edwin Phelps and met father who insisted on taking him back as billetor had written complaining letter.' On the weekend of 6 November Dorothy Hoyles was 'very shocked' to find that four children were returning on the charabanc that had brought their parents from Camberwell on a visit. Two were returning (one despite his father's disapproval) because they were needed to help with younger children but 'Rose Haywood's father could give no reason except

Christmas was a vulnerable time for children with fathers away in the forces. These illustrations were sent by Vanessa Phillips to her father on service in North Africa. (See box on page 150.)

The long road to peace. Two evacuees sit looking down the street of the village where they may remain, parted from their home and family, for several years.

that her mother wanted to see her', and indeed no parents had 'any complaints, only a great wish to have the children back'. At the end of November Miss Hoyles wrote to various wavering parents to try to persuade them not to take their offspring back to London, and dangled the carrot of 'cheap excursion fares from London on 10th December' and activities and parties planned for the children over Christmas, which turned out to include 'festivities and activities (such as carol singing, country dancing, games and reading) 10–12 and 1.30–3.30; also many outdoor treats', a trip to the cinema, 'Christmas frolics' and a party attended by the Mayor and Mayoress of Weymouth with a Christmas tree and a 'Christmas present for every little one in the hall', all of which might have assuaged the homesickness of some of the children but certainly extended the duties of the staff.

But despite official exhortations and propaganda, visits from the Queen to evacuated schools intended to stiffen sinews, and the valiant efforts of teachers, the tide of returnees seemed impossible to stem. By January 1940 it was estimated that nearly 60 per cent of those evacuees who had left in September had returned home.

3   The battle for Britain

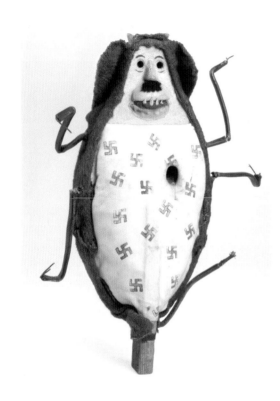

A home-made 'squander bug' copied from government posters that urged people to save for the war effort rather than helping Hitler by 'squandering' their money on consumer goods.

Whit Sunday fell on 12 May in 1940. It was a 'glorious day' and a party of Camberwell parents came down to visit their children in Weymouth. Unfortunately:

> As the charabanc was about to start on its return journey Mr Hunter (59 Corporation Road) billetor of the Maynard children, arrived at the car park, very cross saying that Mrs Maynard, who had hospitably been invited to Mr and Mrs Hunter's home for dinner, was drunk and refused to leave the house in order to catch the bus home.

Peace was finally restored – 'after a few blows had been exchanged between parent and billetors' – and the Camberwell parents departed.

It was an unwelcome complication at an increasingly anxious time. Two days earlier, on 10 May 1940, German tanks had crossed into Holland and Belgium. The war wasn't 'phoney' any more – nor had it been since the German invasion of Denmark and Norway in April. That evening Miss Hoyles and her staff had sent the children back to their billets clutching ARP leaflets warning that gas masks should be checked and repaired if necessary; the government had given orders that in future they must be carried everywhere. The next day identity discs were inspected and more children arrived from London, their parents disquieted by the gravity of the situation. When the headmistress gave the signal for an air-raid warning at assembly she was pleased to note that her pupils managed to clear the church within half a minute, though one little boy had forgotten his gas mask and had to be sent home for it.

By 15 May Holland had surrendered and German forces were pouring into France, and seemingly meeting little resistance. On 20 May the Germans reached the French coast. Suddenly Britain seemed very vulnerable and the English Channel perilously narrow as the German 'blitzkrieg' (lightning war) swarmed on into France. Pleasant English seaside resorts that had seemed so much safer for children than the cities now seemed particularly at risk. A zone ten miles inland along the coast from Norfolk to Sussex was designated a restricted area: all residents who did not have an essential reason to stay were urged to leave and were issued with passes to go in and out; anyone who tried to enter a restricted zone without permission was liable to arrest. London children who had been evacuated to this part of the coast in 1939 were re-evacuated to somewhere it was hoped would be safer from what had begun to seem a very real threat. In the House of Commons the Labour MP and government goad, Josiah Wedgwood, had asked pointedly:

Above: At least until 1942 Britain was fighting a defensive war. The defence was of democracy and freedom of speech, but it was also of a way of life, and artists were employed to remind people of what they might value of their national heritage and be prepared to take up arms to defend. Frank Newbould's painting of 'Alfriston Fair' in Sussex showing children having Bank Holiday fun was one such peacetime scene.

Left: Far horizons. A Brixham, Devon, sailor spins tales of the sea to two London evacuees.

Channel Islands refugees

'We are worried. Having made our home in Guernsey and collected many things we treasure highly,' wrote Mary Trotter on 18 June 1940, 'the Air Force and all the military people seem to be packing up' to leave the Channel Islands, which lie only about 20 miles west of the Cherbourg peninsula. Later that day her son 'brought a form home [from school] to be signed if we were willing to have him evacuated with the other boys'.

The next day it was:
> decided to evacuate children from ... schools, then mothers and young children, others if boats are available. ... There is a somewhat helpless and alarmist feeling about being quite undefended as we looked across the French coast and realised that it was in the hands of the Nazis. ... My son brought home a list of things he must take and I got this ready.

On 20 June Mrs Trotter:
> got my son off with his suitcase. ... There was a feeling that the Germans might arrive at any minute.

> The schoolboys left that afternoon. Many sat on the deck all night. They reached Weymouth at about 7 a.m ... and later that afternoon travelled by special train to Oldham. They were met by buses and taken to a cinema and dance hall converted into a temporary billet.

On 21 June Mary Trotter heard:
> on every side the question 'Are you going?' and mothers and children were leaving all day. ... We heard afterwards that three children were born on the journey and there was much misery and discomfort. ... It was a very strange and upsetting day. ... Tomato boats weren't being loaded: evacuees must come before tomatoes, so tomatoes were given away free. ... everyone had tomato soup that night. ... It has been posted up outside the Education Office that all children had got away safely without accident. ... We are still undecided whether to go or stay.

The Trotters finally decided to join their son in England. On 28 June they:
> got down to the quay at about 6.45. ... Shortly after getting on the boat ... we were startled by two terrific explosions, followed by machine gun fire; then a terrible bombardment started. ... There was no panic, even the children didn't cry. ... We saw ... lorries blazing, the ... wharf a mass of flames and smoke; and heard of other damage and casualties. It was a dreadful piece of brutality on an unprotected island. ... [We] sailed about 10 o'clock wearing life jackets, a very crowded boat. We luckily got across safely and arrived in London on the afternoon of the 29th.

Forty-four Channel Islanders were killed in the air raid. On 30 June German troops started to occupy the Islands – the only British territory to be under German occupation. By then some 30,000 people had got away, but twice that number remained and lived under an increasingly harsh regime, with some 2,000 British civilians sent to German internment camps – and with local officials collaborating in rounding up and deporting Jews to Nazi concentration camps.

Above: Channel Island children safe in Britain sort out shoes sent from the United States.

Has the government prepared any plans to combat the invasion of this country? … I think the fleet can save us from starvation, but not from invasion. … The fact that we did not [manage to save Norway from invasion] makes it very easy to imagine a similar thing happening on the coast of Lincolnshire and the Wash.

The invasion of the Low Countries had made Mary Datchelor School's corner of Kent:

uncomfortably near to the battle front. Throughout May and early June we had various air-raid warnings, and spent some time in the trenches; and we had many telephone conversations with London about our position. But the Authorities in London told us to stay where we were – so we stayed.

That year's school play, *The Barretts of Wimpole Street*, 'was produced to the sound of gunfire from the Channel ports and of aeroplanes overhead'.

On 26 May 1940 the order went out for the total evacuation from Dunkirk of the soldiers of the British Expeditionary Force who had been fighting in France. Between 27 May and 4 June when the evacuation was officially halted, 338,226 men arrived in British ports, though thousands more lay dead or seriously injured or had been taken prisoner in France, and some 2,000 had been killed crossing the Channel. Among the evacuees were around 118,000 French soldiers. At 12.30 p.m. on 31 May 1940, Miss Hoyles:

received a notice by hand that 15,000 French soldiers from Dunkirk were expected in Weymouth and schools were to be closed and all staff to be on duty to work canteens for the French troops. From 1st–14th June inclusive all schools to be closed during occupation of premises by French troops and subsequent cleaning and disinfecting of school premises until the MoH [Medical Officer of Health] passed the schools as fit for children. All teachers on duty and working day and night during the actual occupation and later remaining on call with a skeleton staff on duty at the canteen centre. Windows of school strapped with cellophane [to stop glass splintering in case of shells or bomb blasts].

But despite the dramas unfolding across the Channel and the 'regular patrols of the beach' undertaken by teachers anxious about invasion, life went on much as usual for Albany Road Junior School, with home visits to check up on reported cases of scabies, bed-wetting and bad behaviour. The children enjoyed a bonus of two lesson-free weeks as their teachers ministered to the needs of the French, whose government under the newly-appointed Marshal Pétain surrendered to Hitler's forces on 22 June 1940.

It was Dunkirk that made the teenaged Geoff Tinsey wonder, as he watched the returning soldiers ('some of them in a pretty poor shape') coming ashore from the naval craft and 'little ships' that had put them ashore in his home town of Dover, 'well if this is war, what more's to come? It was a salutary lesson – up to then I think most of us youngsters had thought it was all great fun.' Geoff and his friends volunteered to help in a house-to-house collection for food and clothing for the men, most of whom had only

'I felt as though I were walking with destiny...' A doll made in the image of Winston Churchill, who succeeded Neville Chamberlain as Prime Minister on 10 May 1940, and also took the title – and role – of Minister of Defence.

63

After Dunkirk: Exhausted French soldiers (Cromwell Rd School)

the clothes they stood up in, and were exhausted almost beyond sleep, hungry, thirsty, cold and often soaking wet. Many were traumatised by the ordeal they had suffered in France, the struggle they had had to get on a boat, and the loss of comrades who had not made it. These raggle-taggle soldiers were also anxious about the reception they would receive in England. After all, as Winston Churchill, who had recently replaced Chamberlain as Prime Minister, was to say, while praising the soldiers' courage, 'wars are not won by evacuation'.

Their concerns were groundless: the reception was ecstatic. The defeated army was accorded a heroes' welcome. As his boat reached the coast of Kent, John Curley of the Royal Army Service Corps:

> felt degraded … really at rock bottom, at zero. We couldn't believe what had happened to us, we thought we were the British Army retreating from the Continent which had never happened before like that. We didn't want to meet the people of Dover, we didn't want to meet the people of anywhere on the coast because we were frightened that they would simply throw stones at us. That is what I imagined. … [But] in Dover they put the gangplanks on board and we came down to the most magnificent reception I've ever seen in my life. The ladies of Dover and all the people of Dover were clapping and cheering us and the kids were waving flags, and we couldn't believe it because we'd lost, we'd been kicked out of France by a really efficient German Army. We couldn't believe that these people were welcoming us home like this. … It boosted our morale right to the top, and I thought, 'With people like this behind us how the hell can we lose the war?'

All the way back to London, 'the whole 70 miles of railway track was lined with people on both sides clapping and cheering us. Every time we stopped there were cups of tea passed to us.' Children ran alongside the soldiers' trains as they pulled into stations, passing cups of tea and glasses of lemonade and 'smokes' through the windows of the locked carriages.

Hazel Brown, whose school had been evacuated from south London to Ashford only 11 miles from the coast, was billeted in a house whose 'long narrow garden backed onto allotments and the main railway line from Folkestone to London':

> Every afternoon as soon as I'd finished my dinner and helped wash up, my friends and I went along the road, across the line to a slightly raised area beside the track. Because of its position most of the troop trains passed through Ashford. For several days we stood and watched as they slowly passed along, packed to overflowing with men in khaki, standing, leaning out of the window, they were the fortunate ones

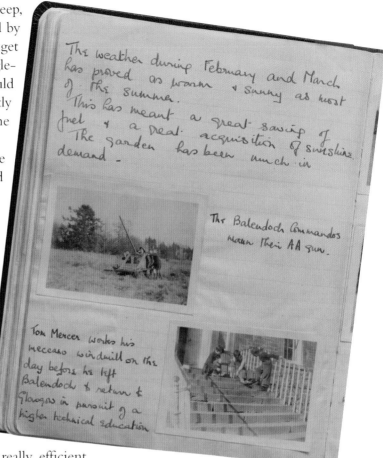

The weather during February and March has proved as warm & sunny as most of the summer.
This has meant a great saving of fuel & a real acquisition of sunshine. The garden has been much in demand –

The Balendoch Commandos man their AA gun.

Tom Mercer works his meccano windmill on the day before he left Balendoch & return to Glasgow in pursuit of a higher technical education

65

Above: Glasgow children evacuated to Balendoch Hostel, Perthshire, take an interest in the Balendoch commandos manning their anti-aircraft guns in the grounds.

Opposite: 'After Dunkirk: Exhausted French Soldiers' in the playground of Cromwell Road School in Weymouth, where the teachers and evacuees of Albany Road School, Camberwell, who were also using the facilities, helped care for them.

Toys of war. A child's Frog model interceptor fighter airplane kit proclaims 'British Made Throughout'.

who'd been rescued from Dunkirk. Sometimes they stood for what seemed hours. We were just youngsters and had nothing, no money to give, but we waved and called Hallo. Lots of the men waved back and some threw postcards or letters out of the windows, asking us to post them so that their wives and families would know that they were safe. A few grownups took baskets along with apples to share. We knew something really important was happening and felt part of it.

Brian Poole was camping with the Boy Scouts when:

The Scout Master woke us up at 5 in the morning to say that 2,500 of the BEF were arriving that morning at a certain place five miles away. Of course we were only too glad to put up tents – 400 in number. I shall never forget those men all my life. All smiling, not a grumble, some had only the clothes they stood up in. I talked to some of them. They all said as man for man we whacked the Germans but we had not enough aeroplanes; they were bombed 18 hours out of 24. One chap said he never saw a British plane. We are all now resolved to give the Germans Hell!!! and we'll fight like that too.

'How now stands France?' Two little girls stand gazing out across the Channel through the coils of anti-invasion barbed wire that was woven along much of the coastline of south-east England in the summer of 1940.

67

Hitler had hoped that after the fall of France Britain would sue for peace, leaving him free to pursue his conquest of Eastern Europe. But Winston Churchill in a speech to the House of Commons had already made it clear that:

> We shall go on to the end. … We shall defend our island whatever the cost may be. We shall fight on the beaches, we shall fight on the landing grounds, we shall fight in the fields and in the streets, we shall fight in the hills, we shall never surrender.

Hitler's commanders had warned him that no invasion could be contemplated unless the RAF was wiped out so that it could not mount a significant attack on any German attempt to cross the Channel. With Luftwaffe planes able to arrive from bases in France in six minutes, southern England was thus in the front line of a German offensive. In the phrase Churchill coined, the 'Battle of Britain' was about to begin. Attacks on shipping and raids on south coast ports would build up by August to *Adlertag* (Eagle Day), an all-out German assault to gain air superiority over southern England and undermine morale by attacks on airfields in a triangle stretching from Stanmore north of London to

Games of war. **Punch** *7 July 1940.*

"*All right, one more Heinkel, Master George—and then down you go.*"

A small boy sits on a German mine washed up on Deal beach in 1941.

Hampshire and across Surrey, Sussex, Essex and Kent to Suffolk.

Winifred Beer was in the sixth form of Portsmouth Southern Secondary School for Girls when it was evacuated to Salisbury on 1 September 1939. When news of the fall of France came through, her foster parents, Mr and Mrs Parson:

> were very agitated. ... Mrs Parson changed a lot of pound and ten shilling notes into silver coins – half crowns and florins – as she observed that silver would still hold its value. They were stored in the garage. Petrol was rationed but some was also stored in the garage so that if we were invaded she would get in the car with the money and drive as far north as possible.
>
> The Parsons set up a target in the garden and they had an airgun. We used to practise shooting as the idea was we would shoot down any German paratroopers.

'We shall fight them in the fields.' A young girl picking hops in the fields of Kent and wearing a tin hat as she does so watches a 'dog fight' between British and German fighter planes in the sky above in September 1940.

Brian Poole was 16 that summer, and had just left his grammar school in Northwick, Cheshire, to start a business course at a Manchester college, on 20 June 1940. He wrote to his American pen friend Trudie (Gertrude Lach):

> Now for it, we're expecting it any time now. Bombs, parashootists [sic] anything. We're fighting with our backs to the wall, only us left to defend democracy. Any invader who sets foot on British soil is for it, instant death, no mercy. ... When your [sic] at Atlantic City remember me, I hope I shall be shooting parashootists down and throwing hand grenades about, you never know. I'll be 17 on Wednesday next and old enough to join the Local Defence Volunteers. I broke the news gradually to mother two nights ago that I was contemplating joining. She thinks I'm too young to fight but I ... pointed out boys of 16 had to fight in the Spanish Civil War ... [and] in South Africa you are liable to be called up at 17. I think that I'm gradually winning her over.

The Local Defence Volunteers (LDV), who at Churchill's insistence were later renamed the Home Guard, had been established when Anthony Eden, the Secretary of State for War, spoke in a broadcast immediately after the 9 o'clock news on 14 May 1940

A German Heinkel He111 bomber, shot down over south-east England during the Battle of Britain, is toured round the country to raise money for Beaverbrook's 'Spitfire Fund.'

about an opportunity for those 'countless ordinary citizens, especially those not eligible to enrol in the armed forces, who had asked to be allowed to serve in the defence of their country in its hour of peril.' The nation wanted:

> large numbers of men who are British citizens between the ages of 17 and 65 to come forward now and offer their services. ... The name of the new force ... describes its duties in three words: Local Defence Volunteers. You will not be paid but you will receive uniforms and you will be armed. In order to volunteer, all you have to do is give your name and address to your local police station, and when we want you, we will let you know.

Almost at once, queues several deep started to form outside police stations and within 24 hours of the appeal 250,000 men had put down their names. Although most of the volunteers were ex-servicemen, there were a number of boys like Brian Poole who wanted to 'do their bit' in Britain's darkest hour, although at under 18 years of age they were too young to enlist in the forces. At first – indeed for some time – their only 'uniform' was an brassard (armband) with the letters LDV stencilled on it, and weapons were in desperately short supply. Recruits drilled with brooms rather than rifles, and almost their only defence against invading Germans, apart from perhaps one First World War Lee Enfield rifle for a platoon, was made up of whatever arcane weapons they might be able to plunder from Cadet Corps or even museums. Kitchen knives lashed to broom handles, pitchforks, garden spades, nails banged into lengths of wood, cricket bats, air rifles and 'Molotov cocktails' – milk bottles filled with an explosive mixture that were to be lobbed at approaching tanks – were about all that most patrols could muster for some time. But this did not dim the enthusiasm of the young (or older) volunteers – there was even an Eton College Anti-Parachutist Observer Corps – as they marched, drilled, presented arms and set out on night-time patrols to defend their country. Eddie Mathieson also joined the Home Guard:

> The very last line of defence. … Ye had tae volunteer. You could join at 15 year old. It was young boys and old men, that was what the Home Guard was comprised of. … [He joined] the Edinburgh battalion. … All the Edinburgh Home Guard wore the Royal Scots cap badge. My dad was in the Home Guard as well. … The … trainin' really was invaluable to me. We saw no action of course. We spent our time plowtering around on golf courses. We could throw hand grenades, dismantle a hand grenade, take a Lewis gun to bits with a blindfold on, things like that.

What the Home Guard was particularly on the alert for were parachutists. Stories of the ease with which Holland and Belgium had been taken by armed soldiers dropping from the skies led to the not illogical expectation that thousands of airborne troops would soon be landing in Britain. Furthermore, according to wild rumours about what had happened on the Continent, these soldiers were most likely to come in disguise, dressed perhaps as nuns or clergymen, or even as British soldiers. Their arrival would be helped by thousands of supposed 'fifth columnists', traitors who, it was feared, would guide the enemy parachutes and gliders to a safe landing and link up with them, participating in acts of sabotage and vicious fighting as the vanguard of Hitler's invasion of Britain.

Brian Poole, who had been a keen maker of model airplanes in peacetime, had resolved that 'now the war's to be taken seriously, it's no time for a boy old enough to fight to go flying model planes.' On 4 August 1940, he was able to write to his pen friend in the US with:

This child found a blind

Accidents occur daily with blinds left on ranges. Report all blinds for destruction at the end of the day's work.

71

Above: Poster warning against the danger of children getting killed when they picked up unexploded mines or hand grenades – as tragically happened on many occasions during the Second World War. Abram Games designed this poster as a warning to those working in munitions factories and testing ranges where explosive substances were tested and used.

Below: Toys of war: a jigsaw showing a pilot in the cockpit of his fighter plane.

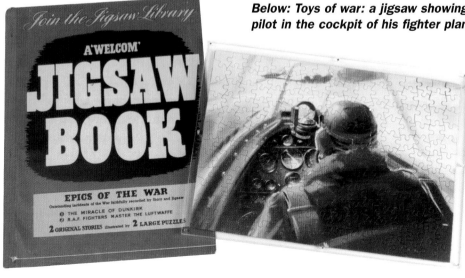

72

'Saucepans – and colanders, frying pans, preserving pans, mugs, fish slices, ladles – and a tin bath – for Spitfires'. Boys help collect aluminium scrap in the belief that it will make a valuable contribution to building fighter aircraft.

the best news yet, I am in the Home Guard (ex Local Defence Volunteers). I've had three rifle drills up to now and I do my first duty from 9 p.m. to 6 a.m. on Wednesday, three hours duty, the rest a sleep on the floor ready for action. [He and a friend were] hoping to be in the fight right pronto!!! What we want is not to shoot the Bosche but to bayonet him. That which the Germans don't like, cold steel. The General in command said our motto will be 'Kill the Bosche' and shoot to kill. Done a fine bit of work today, cleaned 20 rifles with dad [who had fought in the First World War and now, as a section leader of the Home Guard, was pleased to 'find that all his rifle drill has come back to him']. Not so bad, eh? Our house is simply littered with field dressings, supplies of uniforms, steel helmets, ammunition and I don't know what.

Soon the belligerent teenager was able to report:

We have got mother knitting fast for us now, balaclava helmets, mittens, pullovers, scarves, everything for the cold winter nights when dad and I are out at the post. By the by those steel helmets we wear nearly press my head through my shoulders.

In September 1940 Brian, who was by now an accountancy student, had been obliged to give up the Boy Scouts and his membership of the Air Defence Cadet Corps in favour of the Home Guard which took up a minimum of three nights a week and most of Saturday. 'We have been on manoeuvres all this afternoon with the Home Guard,' he wrote on 20 September. 'First day in my army boots COR!! each one weighs about a ton I should think.' Within a month, however, the youthful Home Guard's feet were 'now hardened to heavy army boots' as his unit did:

> a two-hour march every weekend. … It's very exciting learning how to advance in short rushes, bayonet charging. We have had grand instruction on bayonets from Dad. Where to stick it, in the throat, in the lungs or in the stomach giving it a twist as you pull it out. Things like this I would never have done before the war. But now nothing would give me greater pleasure to cut of [sic] a Hun's throat. When we get in more training, we shall manoeuvre with the army and have tanks, artillery and aeroplanes cooperating with us.

Families in Belfast, Northern Ireland, cheer their success in collecting scrap iron for the war effort.

Since late May, children had been being moved out from seaside towns such as Margate; the 'danger map' of Britain had changed and it was now the south of England rather than the big cities that were in the firing line. Some 25,000 children who had been evacuated to Norfolk, Suffolk, Essex, Kent and Sussex, and in many cases had at last begun to settle, were moved again. As soon as they had gone, the schools in the coastal zone were closed in an attempt to encourage local children to leave. If they did not go, they received no education, for as long as four months in some cases.

The country was soon criss-crossed with children on the move. Thirteen towns along the coastal belt were designated as 'evacuable' and as many children as possible were sent to South Wales and the Midlands, while parents whose children had remained in London were strongly advised – again – to send them away. Similar activity was taking place in the Medway towns, Portsmouth, Southampton and Gosport. On 7 July 1940 the exodus started from Newcastle, Middlesbrough, Hull, Grimsby, Gateshead, South Shields, Tynemouth and other towns along the north-east coast.

A notebook kept by K.W. Booker when he was a teenage member of the Home Guard based at Gillingham in Kent.

At the end of June, mindful of the disasters of the official evacuation of mothers and babies back in September 1939, the government cautiously introduced a new 'assisted private evacuation' scheme by which mothers with children under five years of age could make their own arrangements for accommodation in a reception area. They were given free travel vouchers and the government agreed to pay billeting allowances to the householders, whether they were family, friends or strangers. Older children could be taken too, provided they were still going to school.

In late May and early June, Mary Datchelor School lost 60 to 70 girls, whose parents felt that the invasion of that part of Kent was no longer just a remote possibility.

> Finally, on June 18th they took calmly and cheerfully the news that we were again on the move – this time to 'somewhere in Wales'; and on June 23rd, at less than a week's notice, we were moved to Carmarthenshire. ... We had a splendid journey, though as we went through the outskirts of London, not far from our homes, we had some homesick moments; and as the day wore on began to feel very far away. Everywhere we were greeted by waving crowds, and when we stopped at various stations the WVS brought us cups of water and tea and chocolate and newspapers. ... Once more we did not get to the destination originally scheduled for us – Carmarthen – but were taken to Llanelli, where we arrived at 7.30 in a lovely evening light, and had a wonderful welcome. Llanelli is an industrial town of

BESTWAY
LEAFLET 877 3ᵈ

SAILOR, SOLDIER AND AIRMAN DOLLS
(From oddments of 4-ply wool)

Knit your own serviceman. 'Next time Daddy's home on leave he'll have some competition!' advises this knitting pattern which used 'oddments of 4-ply wool' – khaki, air force blue, or navy.

40,000 inhabitants; and its cinemas and Woolworth's were loudly cheered by each bus-load of girls on our arrival.

School life would still be 'a complicated jigsaw' with teaching for the 368 girls spread over five different buildings, but there was the compensation of 'sea (not safe, alas, for bathing) and lovely country within easy reach. ... Many girls had bicycles (we had brought nearly 200 from Ashford) and could go further afield.'

Betty Helliar was still in Peters Green in Bedfordshire, where her school had been evacuated from London:

Every lunch hour [as] the Germans advanced across Holland, Belgium and France, [I] used to hurry round the corner to a radio shop and stand in a group on the pavement to hear the latest news. ... With the fall of France, the authorities decided to put into effect the second evacuation of children. This was very different from the first. ... On the day fixed for travel, owing to the gravity of the situation, more children turned up than had registered. No one was excluded.

My party went by train to Melksham, a lovely little country town in Wiltshire. It was a *very* hot day and just before the train started helpers came along the platform with mugs and buckets of water for the children to have a drink. Alas my party did not get any because we had been shown into the Guard's van. We could

The official War Artist Edward Ardizzone's gentle portrait of a village 'Dad's Army', entitled 'An Evening Parade of the LDV in their Early Days.'

not sit down on the journey as the floor was dirty and smelt of fish. (We could not blame the railway – every moveable train was pressed into service that day.)

Church Road School was housed in the local Melksham British Legion club.

> Another teacher and I formed the staff. … The club used the ground floor and we had the upper floor. It was furnished with a piano and a blackboard, and had chairs with slotted seats, we also had some stock – paper and books. The other teacher and I … discussed what our curriculum might be, obviously lots of music [since the other teacher 'was a very good pianist']; we couldn't do much in the way of drill because we didn't think the floor would stand it. Writing was difficult as we had no desks. Sometimes the children knelt on the floor and wrote on the seats of the chairs, but as they were slatted, the pencils kept going through the spaces. We could not go for walks with the children because Melksham was a busy town. It was an unorthodox school but the children seemed happy and worked hard.

Even before war started various Commonwealth countries had offered to take British children as evacuees. Southern Rhodesia offered refuge, as did a Canadian's women's

If the invasion comes...

In July 1940 invasion fever was at a high pitch, and it periodically revived over the next year. A government-issued leaflet advised the population to hide food, maps, bicycles, petrol – any conceivable thing that could aid an invader. 'Join Britain's Silent Column' posters warned about 'loose talk' that might give away secrets to the enemy. People were told to be on the alert for 'anything suspicious', while German parachutists were widely expected to drop from the skies – maybe dressed as nuns and carrying collapsible bicycles.

The Home Guard was taking no chances. The unscrupulous 'Jerry' would stop at nothing, even involving children in their deadly ruses. This 1941 exercise (left) was an example of such wilder shores of a beleaguered island's imagination. Members of the Home Guard challenge a suspicious looking 'nursemaid' pushing a pram. The dastardly enemy agent pulls out a gun, but the Home Guard are more than his equal; they fell the enemy and tip over the pram, which is fortunately empty.

'A proper army now.' *A three-year-old child watches her father polish the brass buttons on his greatcoat before going on night duty with the Home Guard.*

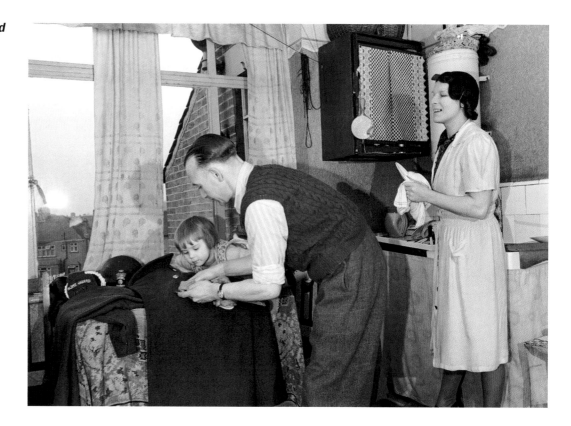

78

organisation which was prepared to take those who were under 16 or over 60, and Australia offered a home for orphans for the duration of the war. The British government rejected the invitations as 'good-hearted but impractical' since it was concerned that such an exodus overseas might look like defeatism. Indeed in the darkest days of the war, rumours frequently circulated that the royal family had gone to Canada (which of course they never did) as a measure of how desperate things were.

But there was nothing to stop people from sending their children out of England if they could afford the fare (£15 for a passage to the United States, or roughly a month's salary for some three-quarters of the working population) and had family or friends in the Dominions or America who were prepared to take them for the duration. And many did.

The socialite Conservative MP Henry 'Chips' Channon sent his son to America, and the pacifist writer Vera Brittain sent her son and her daughter (who would grow up to be the Liberal Democrat politician, Shirley Williams). Duff Cooper, a wartime Minister of Information, and his wife, Lady Diana, sent their son, John Julius Norwich, a diplomat and writer in later life. Another 'seavacuee' was Elizabeth Taylor, who would one day be a glamorous, violet-eyed film star. But many lesser luminaries also opted to despatch their children on what in wartime could be a perilous journey overseas.

Joan Zilva was 14 when she was evacuated to Canada. Given what seemed the very real risk in June 1940 of a Nazi invasion of Britain, 'those with Jewish blood would be unlikely to survive'. Dr Zilva, a biochemist 'who was racially but not religiously Jewish', had come to Britain as a refugee from Russian pogroms in 1907. 'My parents did not want (nor would have been allowed) to leave the sinking ship, but decided, against my will, that I should be saved a grisly fate,' so Joan was sent from the family home in Surrey to Canada. As the *Duchess of Atholl* nosed into Montreal harbour, she wrote:

> I just realised last night, and I keep realising now, that I shall not see you or Sanderstead, for at least six months, perhaps more, and I have got to stay here all that time. If it was just a week, perhaps it would not be so bad.

Several weeks later she confessed, 'I *always* feel homesick when I wake up, though I try not to.' It was three years before Joan Zilva was able to persuade her parents to let her return home.

Byron House School was a private co-educational establishment for children aged between two and 14 in Highgate, north London. It decided to go overseas, along with a number of pupils from independent schools, including Abinger Boys' School and Sherborne, Roedean and Benenden girls' schools. On 26 June 1940, by which time 'invasion by the Germans seemed a certainty' in the view of Miss Williams, a teacher at the school, 28 pupils and three teachers set sail from Liverpool to Canada aboard the *Duchess of Atholl*.

> It was a hazardous journey as there were no convoys [as protection against U-boat attacks] in those early days, and we spent one day circling in mid-ocean as a German submarine was in the vicinity. All the children were seasick except one. There were 800 children on board and as the boat had previously been used as a troop carrier, there were very few stewards on board.

'Dear Mummy,' wrote Elizabeth Paish, one of the Byron House School children, who was on her way to Canada with her brother, Anthony:

> The boat started on Thursday. On Friday, it was very rough and I was seasick the whole day: everybody was seasick except Joanna. … We have to take lifejackets about with us in case a U-boat or German submarine came [sic].
> We have meals in a very posh dining room, Elizabeth Rowlatt and I have a table together and there are very different menus for every meal. … We have got a very nice waiter who serves us, his name is Joe. … We have to put the clocks back an hour every day … so we are listening to the 1 o'clock news at twenty past ten. … We did have a destroyer to guard us and another ship, but it has left us now and gone with the other ship. Miss Williams says we will see Canada tomorrow.

One of the first child evacuees to go to the United States with the help of the American Allied Relief Fund on 9 August 1940, kisses his soldier father farewell.

79

80

'Intern them all...'

On the outbreak of the Second World War, every one of the 73,000 German or Austrian refugees in Britain aged 16 or over was deemed a potential 'enemy alien' – despite the fact that many had fled from Nazi oppression – and was ordered to appear before a tribunal whose duty was to order the internment of those it considered potential threats to British security.

In May 1940, with the German invasion of the Low Countries and wild speculation about 'fifth columnists' within Britain poised to assist an invasion attempt, the noose tightened. Various measures culminated in an order on 27 May 1940 that German and Austrian men and women between 16 and 60 whose loyalty was for some reason considered to be in doubt were to be interned. The only exceptions were those who were infirm, in an advanced state of pregnancy or had dangerously ill children.

'Collar the lot,' Churchill had ordered, and when on 10 June 1940 Mussolini declared war on Britain and France, that also meant all Italian men between 17 and 70 who had been resident in Britain for less than 20 years were taken to an internment camp before being transported to the Isle of Man, or the men shipped overseas, since Newfoundland, Canada and Australia had agreed to accommodate internees from Britain. On 25 June 1940 this blanket order was extended to all male Germans and Austrians: now only children under 16 and old men over 70 were to be left at liberty.

Left: Women and children 'enemy aliens' leave with a police escort for an internment camp on 29 May, 1940.

Painting of child internees by Fred Uhlman, who was himself interned on the Isle of Man. An ex-lawyer turned artist, Uhlman painted and drew many vivid illustrations of a life he considered to be worse than that of a common convict, who at least knows when his release will come.

Adolescents found their education summarily interrupted; some arrived at the camps still wearing the school uniform in which they had been arrested. Many young children, who might already have suffered traumas fleeing from Nazi oppression in their home countries, found themselves suddenly fatherless and cared for by a bewildered and anxious mother who had no understanding of why her husband had been marched away, where he had been taken, or for how long he might be away.

When mothers with young children were interned and could not make satisfactory arrangements for their children's care, some took their children with them into the camps. Others left them with relatives or friends and suffered agonies of worry at the enforced separation, and many sent for their children to join them in the camps.

Some 4,000 women were interned, as compared with 23,000 men. Most of the female internees were housed in one of two camps on the Isle of Man, Port Erin or Port Mary, living in small hotels or boarding houses. Two Froebel-trained internees started a nursery school, and the head of a progressive school who had fled from Germany was given charge of the camp school for older children. Boredom was the main complaint. A man who was interned as an 11-year-old remembers, 'We had a lot of handicrafts and we dissected seagulls; there were a lot of them around.'

In answer to a parliamentary question, it was admitted that 300 women were pregnant when they were interned, and many had their babies in the camps.

Internment was an inhumane policy, and criticism was persistent – if muted – but to little avail until 15 July 1940. Then, though no official announcement was ever made, the internment of 'enemy aliens' ceased. Gradually over the next two years the majority of the men, women and youths who had been interned emerged from their barbed-wire captivity to try to live a 'normal' wartime life, and in many cases offer whatever help they could to Britain's war effort.

The school party arrived in Montreal on 5 July and was put on a train to Ottawa. Miss Williams noted that:

> The children were given milk and bread and butter ['which was white and fluffy and not at all like English bread so I had 10 slices,' Elizabeth Paish recalls] [and] after the meal we put each child on a seat and in ten minutes they were all asleep. Not so the Staff, they were not given a moment's peace because passengers and train staff alike kept walking along the coach to bombard us with questions, and we could have had all the children adopted before we reached Ottawa.

A little before midnight, the school party arrived at Elmwood School, a girls' boarding school that had just closed for the summer holidays.

Many of the Byron House children stayed in Canada for over four years, not returning home until August 1944 when victory in Europe seemed assured. During their enforced exile there were many things to delight them. Elizabeth Paish enjoyed seeing chipmunks in the garden, and like her fellow pupils revelled in:

> the long hot, endlessly sunny summer days ... autumn's blazing glory ... and wonderfully white winters of snow boots and snow suits ... and learning to skate on the rink in the garden, pushing a wooden chair for balance ... tobogganing over the icy crust of snow in the woods.

However, the Paish's foster parents:

A telegram and a congratulatory tag sent by Geoffrey Shakespeare, chairman of the Children's Overseas Reception Board, to Shiela Mackay, one of the 321 evacuees on board the Dutch liner SS Volendam when she was hit by a torpedo on 30 August 1940 on her way to Canada. The children took to the lifeboats and all were saved, though sadly the ship's purser died.

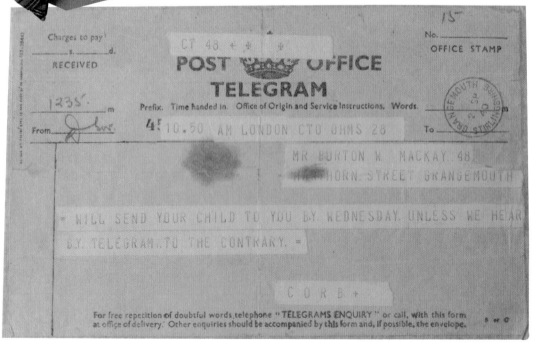

'were more like grandparents than parents [and] we were very in awe of them. ... We had to go to church every Sunday wearing hats and gloves. ... We never became Canadianised; we kept our English accents more or less, and we weren't allowed to drink Coke or take part in 'trick or treat' at Hallowe'en.

It must have been strange for the parents as well as the children when they all got together again. The parents had to make a new relationship with their children. The story was that one parent went up to the wrong child on the station when the children returned – just didn't recognise her own infant! ... [In an attempt to avoid this estrangement Miss Williams] wrote and

'Seavacuees'. Some of the over 400 children and their escorts bound for Australia under the auspices of the CORB evacuation scheme to the Dominions, board their ship at Liverpool.

said would the fathers please write, and would they please send photographs. … The children wrote to their parents every week but after a bit they didn't know quite who they were writing to any more.'

By late May 1940, the threat of invasion seemed sufficiently real for the government to consider a scheme to send children abroad. The initiative was also in the spirit of a 'people's war', in which everyone would be called upon equally to make sacrifices and would in return receive equal shares of scarce resources and equal protection against the enemy. That at least was the theory. It did not quite work like that in a number of areas, and one that had come to seem particularly iniquitous by 1940 was the inability of the less well-off to send their children abroad to safety as their wealthier fellow citizens could.

On 19 June 1940 it was announced in parliament that a Children's Overseas Reception Board (CORB) would be set up under the chairmanship of the new Dominions Parliamentary Under-Secretary, Geoffrey Shakespeare, to accept the renewed offers by the United States, Canada, Australia, New Zealand and South Africa to provide

SS City of Benares

On Friday 13 September 1940, the SS City of Benares set sail from Liverpool. The passenger list included 90 children who were being sent to safety in Canada under the auspices of the government's Children's Overseas Reception Board (CORB) scheme, and another ten whose parents had made private arrangements for them. As the ship pulled away from its berth, the children's voices singing 'Wish Me Luck As You Wave Me Goodbye' wafted back to the parents waving on the quayside.

Four days out in the choppy Atlantic Ocean, the naval escort accompanying the convoy (of which the Benares was the lead ship) was called away, and the convoy sailed on alone. At 10.30 p.m. on 17 September, with a Force Eight gale blowing, a torpedo fired by a U-boat struck the ship just below the cabins where the CORB children were asleep in their bunks. Two children were killed instantly, and the order was given to abandon ship soon after. Only half an hour after being hit, the Benares sank beneath the waves. It was a bitterly cold, rain-lashed night, and several lifeboats were smashed as they hit the rough sea.

That dreadful night, children and adults were swept from lifeboats, or lost their grip on the upturned hulks they had been clinging onto. The only lights were occasional flashes from one of the lifeboats, and in the freezing, inky blackness of the mid-Atlantic, survivors among the ten men and women who had been employed as CORB escorts sang, told stories, anything to keep the children awake until morning when help would surely come.

But as morning dawned, the sea was empty. Nothing could be seen except the sea and a few wave-tossed lifeboats. The captain of the destroyer HMS Hurricane had been alerted to the disaster soon after the Benares had been hit, but the ship was 200 miles away and the storm made progress slow; it was not until the early afternoon that the destroyer came alongside the first of the lifeboats. In one, 21 children lay dead; in others a few survivors lay barely alive with bodies around them. They had been in the open boats or in the water for 19 hours; they were dehydrated, their clothes were sodden, and they were suffering from hypothermia when they were gently winched aboard the Hurricane.

Their parents, who believed that they had sent their children to a safe place as the Blitz raged over Britain, were devastated to receive a letter from CORB on 20 September:

The ship carrying your child/children to Canada was torpedoed on Tuesday night, 17 September. I am afraid that your child/children is/are not amongst those reported as rescued, and I am informed that there is no chance of their being any further ... survivors.

In fact, in what seemed a near miracle, there were more survivors. For eight days, 46 people including six CORB boys and two of their escorts had been rowing as hard as they could, sustained by the determination of one of the escorts, Mary Cornish, a 41-year-old music teacher. They were sighted by a Sunderland flying boat and HMS Anthony was despatched to rescue them.

The death toll was 256: 122 crew and 134 passengers, 81 of them children, including five from a single family. As the

CORB letter of condolence sorrowfully made clear: 'The course of the war has shown that neither by land nor sea can there be complete safety.'

Left: Members of the crew and children from the SS City of Benares, who survived for eight days adrift in a lifeboat, aboard HMS Anthony, the ship that picked them up.

Right: Children from the SS City of Benares aboard HMS Hurricane, the British destroyer that rescued a number of survivors.

Below right and below: Beryl Myatt was lost at sea when the SS City of Benares was sunk. Here is the birthday card from her mother sent to her a month before the tragedy, and the notice of Beryl's death.

Daily Express

Monday, September 23, 1940   One Penny

Sent to escape the bombers, 89 English children are murdered by a U-boat

CHILDREN'S LINER SUNK WITHOUT WARNING IN GALE

An angel took my flower away,
But I will not repine,
For Jesus in His bosom wears
The flower that once was mine.

Happy Birthday GREETINGS

Your Birthday makes us
all 'look up',
And in our doggie way,
We wish you lots of
Birthday Joys
Upon this Happy Day!

In Loving Memory of

BERYL,

Dearly beloved daughter of Tom and Emmie,

Lost at sea, September 17th, 1940,

Aged 9 years.

wartime homes for large numbers of evacuees from Britain.

When CORB headquarters opened for business the next morning, an estimated 3,000 people were waiting to register their children for the scheme and all day more arrived. The scheme was publicised in the press with parents asked to:

> decide whether they will face the pain of not seeing their own children for perhaps years, when they are at the most important stage in their young lives, but knowing that they are growing up safe from Nazi bombers, from death, injury, and that youthful minds will not be forever contaminated by total warfare.

By 4 July, 211,448 applications for children to be sent overseas under the CORB scheme had been received. The children's passage would be free, though most parents would be required to contribute to their child's maintenance as they would if he or she had been evacuated within Britain, and parents with children at fee-paying schools would be expected to pay £1 a week towards the children's upkeep and contribute £15 towards their travel costs.

In contrast to home evacuation, there was no government pressure to send children overseas. Indeed, Winston Churchill was implacably opposed to the scheme, regarding it as 'encouraging a defeatist spirit'. Parents were required to sign a form indemnifying the government against responsibility for their children's safety, and no commitment to bring them back at any specific time was given. Nevertheless, the number of parents who were apparently prepared to risk an ocean crossing at a time when U-boats were sinking Allied shipping amazed the government. Britain did not have anything like the shipping capacity to transport the number of children whose parents were apparently eager for them to depart Britain's shores. Two weeks after the scheme had been introduced, the application lists were closed. Disgruntled Labour MPs demanded an explanation. Had it all been a con? A meaningless gesture to assuage public opinion? A promise to working-class parents that the government had never intended to keep?

The scheme had been 'suspended' not abandoned, Geoffrey Shakespeare insisted, and CORB continued to grant exit visas to those parents who were able to make private arrangements and were prepared to take the risk. But while some 4,200 children (accompanied by 1,100 adults) went to the United States and around 13,000 to Canada under private arrangements, only 2,650 children were CORB seavacuees.

On 17 September 1940, tragedy was layered over muddle-headedness when the SS *City of Benares*, which had set off from Liverpool for Canada four days earlier, was torpedoed in mid-Atlantic. Seventy-seven CORB evacuees perished with six of their escorts, 51 other passengers and 122 crew members. On 3 October the scheme was finally stopped, though exit visas continued to be granted to parents who were able to make their own arrangements for their children.

★ ★ ★

Though he later recognised that the Battle of Britain was 'Britain's finest hour' as the RAF fought valiantly to maintain mastery of the skies, Robert Edom, who was seven in 1940 and living on the outskirts of London, found it:

The Promised Land: British evacuees climb the rigging aboard SS Samaria to get a better view of their home 'for the duration' as they sail into New York harbour on 14 October 1940.

Wartime overseas

Anne Wallace went to stay with relatives in Alaska with her mother and sister in November 1940.

Right: A Christmas card showing Anne, her mother and sister with her US family.

Below right: A letter Anne wrote to her father back in England:

Dear Dear Daddy
do you know that we see the same moon, the sun the stars as you? I eat the same kind of marmalade as you. Daddy I might be home before Christmas. Daddy I made an apron and a pretty yellow bonnet all by myself. I love you. Hugs and kisses from Anne

Below: Anne (centre) at nursery school under a portrait of the American President George Washington.

a bit of a swizz. It was just vapour trails in the sky and the distant rattle of real machine guns. The rest I learnt from my mum's *Daily Express* or the 9 o'clock news when Alvar Lidell or Bruce Belfrage used to rattle on about the number of [German planes] shot down as if they were cricket scores.

For many children in southern England, what has become known as the 'Spitfire Summer' seemed a great deal more immediate than a report in the newspapers or on the wireless as Goering's Luftwaffe switched its assault inland. 'Hordes of German bombers were coming over. They often seemed so low that you could almost touch them. Like great horrible black beetles protected by their fighters with our fighters trying to get in amongst them and shoot them down.'

One woman who, as a four-year-old child in 1940, lived near Biggin Hill airfield, a prime target in the front line throughout the Battle of Britain, recalls that summer:

> We could never seem to get away from the screaming noise of the planes and the bullets and the shrapnel falling. … I would run from the house to the shelter with my mum holding a dustbin lid over my head, but even four feet underground with coats and blankets wrapped round my head, it was deafening.

'It was like watching a war film' as planes wove around the sky, zooming down and letting rip bursts of machine gunfire, recalls Ron Cox who was about to sit his School Certificate exams in Kent. A master strode into the examination hall and instructed the pupils, 'Don't waste time looking out of the windows. If you hear anything falling, you can always get under the desk.'

Peter Tilling, who was 13 when the Battle of Britain started, found it:

> quite exciting really. Sometimes you could actually see the tracer bullets hit the aircraft. They really didn't seem very far away at all and a few times we had airmen coming down with parachutes and I used to get on my bike and go off to try to find them. There was one plane that crashed a few roads away, and I got on my bike and cycled over and picked up a parachute harness as it burned. It was what all boys did at the time, collect souvenirs of the conflict.

As well as collecting souvenirs, boys were soon expert at recognising the planes that screamed and soared overhead. The Penguin book *Aircraft Recognition* was a wartime best-seller, and the degree of technical knowledge of even young children astonishing. 'Junkers 88,' a six-year-old staying in the same house as the writer Elizabeth Jane Howard, in Sussex, pronounced. 'Eighty-seven,' his same-age friend responded. 'They didn't mention its state or the enormous explosion when it crashed in a neighbouring field.'

Although Hurricanes outnumbered them by roughly three to two, it was Spitfires that fired the imagination of the British public – including its children. And soon there was a way to do more than gasp in admiration as the sun glanced off a Spitfire's graceful fuselage and elliptical wings as the planes darted and twisted in pursuit of German Messerschmitts

Here a small girl rehearses her broadcasting skills in Canada. Evacuees sent overseas would regularly take part in two-way radio programmes with friends and family back home.

and Heinkels high in the sky. One of Churchill's first acts on taking the helm in May 1940 was to appoint his old friend, the Canadian newspaper magnate Lord Beaverbrook, Minister of Aircraft Production to 'ensure that our air crews [were] adequately and properly supplied with whatever type and quantity of equipment they required' for the fight ahead. Beaverbrook had a flair for publicity and he knew his task was not only to step up aircraft production: it was also to boost public morale and hammer home the message that an all-out effort was needed from everyone in the country in that perilous summer of 1940 when Britain's chances of avoiding defeat seemed slender indeed.

Housewives were asked to contribute whatever they could in the way of aluminium saucepans, kettles, frying pans, colanders, zinc baths, anything they could spare – and much they could not – to be melted down to make Spitfires. Children were mobilised to make house-to-house collections of 'Saucepans for Spitfires' and cart the household goods to the huge dumps that soon piled up in every town and city. It was more political gesture than practical policy: housewives parted with goods they would find impossible to replace as the war dragged on, and there was probably all the aluminium needed still for sale in the shops or in scrap merchants' yards. But at a time of danger it gave young and old a feeling that there was at least *something* they could do for their country.

'I am very happy to give this week's pocket money towards a Spitfire. Hoping it will win the war soon,' wrote Bertram Gentry who had been evacuated to Somerset, enclosing a sixpenny bit for the Mayor of Taunton's Spitfire Fund. Picking up on an idea that had originated in Jamaica, where a fund had been set up so people could contribute money to build more planes to fight the Luftwaffe, Beaverbrook announced that it cost £5,000 to build a Spitfire (the true cost was nearer £12,000) and then 'priced' the various parts of the plane. £2,500 would buy the fuselage, the wings cost £1,800, the undercarriage £800 and the guns another £800, but Bertram Gentry's pocket money would have bought a rivet or six screws, and those who could afford a bit more could contribute a roller blind for night flying at 7/6d, a sparking plug for 8/- or 'an audible warning horn' for 10/6d. The money poured in, cities and towns competing with each other to see which could raise the most money; towns, companies or individuals who sent in £5,000 could choose the name of 'their' Spitfire.

In Cardiff two boys raised 10/- for the Fund by spending their summer holidays collecting golf balls, and other children sent in their pocket money to swell the Cardiff total to £20,000: sufficient for four Spitfires. In Penzance in Cornwall, evacuees went blackberrying and sold the fruit for 2d a pound as their contribution; in Hackney, a deprived inner London borough, the children at an elementary school managed to collect 10/- and similar efforts were reported from every part of Britain.

In this way, as in so many others, children were in the front line of the Second World War from the start. But the heart-wrenching poignancy of Britain's 'Spitfire Summer' was how many young men who were barely out of childhood themselves fought and died in the defence of their country. In August 1940, the deadliest month of the Battle of Britain, 230 RAF pilots were killed: their average age was 24.

An article that appeared in a Canadian magazine in November 1940 with photographs by Karsh of Ottawa showing how the children of Byron House School, Highgate, were settling into their new homes in the city.

89

4   Children of the Blitz

'Saturday [7 September 1940] was another beautifully sunny day. I was sunning myself in the garden, dad was playing tennis with his brother (Uncle Fred) around the corner and mum was machining some new curtains (very optimistically as it later emerged). At around 3 o'clock the inevitable air-raid warning sounded but as usual I took no notice. I heard the drone of aeroplanes in the distance and then saw them coming over – hundreds of them. … At first I was quite excited thinking that they were our bombers going out on a raid … until I saw small puffs of black smoke among them. I called to mum to come and have a look and she was coming downstairs as the bombs started to fall. … The only time I had seen anything like this was on the films and I just couldn't believe it was happening to us! We made a quick dive for our shelter as one exploded quite near us, blowing out our windows and scaring the living daylights out of our little fox terrier, Rex. Mind you he wasn't the only one who was scared – mum and I were both terrified.

Shortly afterwards dad came back. He said that the bomb that had shattered our windows had blown him down some steps. It had been a direct hit on an air-raid warden's post killing all the occupants. This was in the next road and much too close for comfort – for us the war had now begun in earnest. … We found Rex trying to get behind the toilet in the bathroom and he was still shaking. He had been cut on his paw so we cleaned him up and took him to the shelter with us. He soon learned what the shelter was for and he often arrived before anyone else. …

The raid continued until around 5 o'clock until the All Clear sounded. It had been three hours of continuous bombing: it all seemed totally unreal to us. … When we finally came out of the shelter the sky was red everywhere and there was an awful smell, which dad said was cordite from the explosives – a smell which was to become very familiar to us. Living as we did so near to the docks, which were obviously the target, we were right in the firing line. We made an attempt to clear up the mess of soot and broken glass. Everywhere outside there was chaos. A few families who had cars were loading them up and driving off. Just as we were trying to take everything in and still not able to believe what had actually happened, the sirens started up again. It must have been around 7 o'clock then, just as dusk began to appear. I felt my stomach churning again.

This time we were in the shelter all night – about 12 hours – with no sleep at all. Bombs were falling all around.'

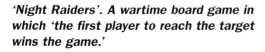

'Night Raiders'. A wartime board game in which 'the first player to reach the target wins the game.'

90

So wrote 17-year-old Florence Rollinson, whose younger sister Lily had been evacuated to Somerset, but who had stayed at home with her parents in Bow in east London. That 'Black Saturday' was the start of the Blitz: the 57 consecutive nights when German planes would drone nightly over London dropping bombs on the capital, and in due course fanning out to attack other provincial towns and cities in an attempt to knock out Britain's war production capacity and break the morale of its people. There were daylight raids too in the early days until aircraft losses grew too high for the Luftwaffe to sustain.

For Bernard Kops, who had returned from evacuation to the tenement building where his extended family lived, leaving Rose behind:

> that day stands out like a flaming wound in my memory. Imagine a ground-floor flat crowded with hysterical women, crying babies and great crashes in the sky and the whole earth shaking. Someone rushed in: 'The docks are alight. All the docks are alight.' I could smell burning.
>   'Trust the poor to get it in the neck, why don't they sort out the rich?'

'Alert at Torry, Aberdeen' painting by Christopher Perkins showing a family making for their Anderson shelter.

91

Ronald McGill was returning from the Oval on the afternoon of the 7 September when:

> over came the German aircraft. I couldn't believe the noise. It was like clouds and clouds of dancing spots in the sunlight, that's the only way I can describe it … and the whole formation had got through to London. I said to Mum, 'They're German.' And she said, 'No, they're not, they're British.' But they weren't of course. We didn't see the actual bombs, we were too far away, but a great pall of smoke went up. It was unbelievable. Then everyone was frightened and people began to run around and these Cockney women were shaking their fists at them, and some had knives, and you name it, what they weren't going to do to Hitler. They were frightened all right but it was the anger of resistance, you know the 'wait till I get my 'ands on 'im' sort of thing, rather than cowardly fear.

At the end of three dreadful hours, Bernard Kops recalls:

> The All Clear sounded a beautiful symphony in [our] ears and everyone relaxed,

the men arguing about politics, the women talking about food. But the younger people wandered out to see the fires and I went with them towards the Commercial Road. The closer I got the more black and red it became, with flames shooting higher than the cranes along the dockside. Sparks were spitting everywhere and tongues of flames consumed the great warehouses along the black and orange water of the Thames. Everything was chaos except the fire which was like a living monster with an insatiable appetite. And I was afraid of being devoured, besides I hated to watch the firemen working so hard so I left by myself and wandered back towards Stepney Green where black smoke covered the sky. ... The smoke made my eyes smart and water. A policeman standing near told me not to cry. 'Don't worry sonny, we're going to beat the hell out of those Germans.' ...

When I got back to the Buildings I could see my mother standing there screaming for her children. ... 'They're coming tonight. Quick! Quick!' ...

I looked out of the window and watched the darkening sky. But the flames took over from the daylight and the whole world was red. The family inquest reached only one conclusion. The Germans had set fire to the docks in order to have a beacon for the coming night of terror. ... 'God is good, we'll get over it.' My mother's faith must have been lined with asbestos. But I couldn't think of getting over it and lived purely in the present, nervously talking to myself, playing the fool, or going to the lavatory several times over. When the sirens wailed the bombers were on their tail. ... I got a strange feeling of loneliness, of being cut off in that lighted room, cut off from all existence. Most of the kids had dropped off to sleep but I lay outstretched on the floor counting the explosions. ... [After the All Clear] I left about seven and wandered around the streets. The war had come home to roost.

People were poking around in the ruins, pulling out a few precious belongings. ... But I didn't have much time to reflect on life and death for a new game was in progress.

The boys of Stepney Green were scrubbing around in the debris near the clock tower for pieces of shrapnel. This caught my imagination and I immediately set to. I found lots of pieces of blue and grey metal and proudly showed them to another kid. 'That bit's no

Left: Clutching their bedding, London families queue up to be let into an underground station to take shelter for the night, September 1940. By the end of the year, a ticketing system had been introduced which put an end to the chaos of unrestricted entry to the tubes.

Below: 'Sketch of an air raid on London'. A watercolour painting by Stephen Macfarlane, aged 12.

9 3

good. It's from an ack-ack gun, but that's all right. That's from a German bomb.' I wondered who made the rules but I played the game. I was very pleased with my shrapnel and I rushed home to show my family who were eating and cleaning up and washing and discussing and arguing and I went out again after breakfast round to Redmans Road to look for some more. In front of me was a space where once had been the house of a boy I knew. Not a very close friend, just someone I played with occasionally.

'What happened?' I asked a warden.

'They all got killed.'

Funny, I thought, I had seen him only the day before and now he was no more.

That first night more than 430 people were killed and some 1,600 seriously injured. It was amazing that there were not more casualties as East Enders surveyed the devastation around the docks and the surrounding areas, where firemen were trying to contain fires that were still burning voraciously as a cold, grey dawn broke over London.

The next night the bombers came back and bombs fell for eight and a half hours. Not until 3 November, when bad weather gave a single night's respite for the capital, would there be one night when the air-raid sirens did not sound. Almost all major incidents involved children: one particularly terrible catastrophe happened on the third night of the London Blitz at South Hallsville School in Canning Town, where hundreds of families who had been bombed out of their homes gathered waiting for transport to take them out of the area. For two days and nights they waited, but the buses never arrived and at 3.45 a.m. on Monday 9 September the school received a direct hit that demolished half the building and brought downs tons of masonry. As rescue workers tried to dig out the wounded, a blackout was imposed and a cordon thrown round the building to keep the terrible sights from the gaze of local residents. There has been dispute ever since about how many died that night. The campaigning journalist Ritchie Calder, who was haranguing the government for the lack of shelter provision for the poor, put the number at 450; the local council's official figure was 73 and they denied persistent local rumours that the bomb site was concreted over with many bodies still unrecovered. But what was tragically indisputable was that many children were killed, including Hazel Chandler aged four and her six-month-old sister Edna, who perished with their father James and mother Eva.

'Now that the raids had really started,' Florence Rollinson's father 'said he thought that I might like to join Lily in Taunton. I said I wasn't going without mum and she said she wasn't going without dad – so we stayed in London.' Although there had been frequent if intermittent raids on London and its environs, and on ports and provincial cities before the Blitz started, there were fewer than half a million children still billeted in safer areas of the country to which they had been evacuated, and many of these had been evacuated from the coastal areas earlier in the summer. This meant that there were, for example, more than 52,000 children of school age in the London evacuation area when the bombers came on 7 September.

It might have been thought that now the attack everyone had been dreading was

Even dolls seemed to need a uniform in wartime. A WAAF (Women's Auxiliary Air Force) toy.

finally happening, there would be a mass exodus from the cities – London in particular. But this did not happen. Around 20,500 unaccompanied children left the capital in September, but as Londoners seemed to get accustomed to the nightly raids, the number of leavers dropped. In December only 766 children left under the auspices of any organised scheme, though more may have gone – or returned – to privately arranged billets under their own steam. Official admonitions and encouragement did not seem to work: too many people had had bad experiences with the first evacuation, and there were many parents for whom the nightmare of the Blitz gave an added reason for the family to stay together. The government reluctantly rejected the idea of compulsory evacuation as unworkable and unacceptable. Authorities were, however, empowered to send away from the Greater London area any child certified to be suffering – or likely to suffer – in mind or body as a result of enemy attacks. But during the whole of 1941 only 470 children, most of them under five, were evacuated under this order.

In late September organised – though voluntary – evacuation of mothers with their children was reintroduced. At first this opportunity was restricted to homeless mothers and children in the East End, but the take-up was so small that the scheme was extended

'Children still playing in Silvertown, September, 1940' by Edward Ardizzone. Silvertown, the area around London's docks, was very heavily bombed on the first night of the Blitz, 7 September 1940, and on many subsequent occasions.

After the raid. Bombed-out families sit among their possessions in the East End in the morning after the raid of 13 September 1940.

96

An ARP warden helps mothers and young children who have been made homeless in an air raid on the East End, to find a place of safety.

to include all mothers with children of any age who wanted to get away. By the end of May 1941, after almost nine months of heavy bombing, fewer than 130,000 mothers and children had evacuated, and over three-quarters of these had left in October 1940.

Six-year-old Barbara Roose lived with her mother and younger brother, Geoff, 'right in the heart of London in Bedfordbury, Covent Garden – five solid, grey, Victorian tenement blocks. ... The residents called it "the Bury" for short.' Her father was in the army, and her mother had declined to send her and Geoff out of London. Barbara continued to attend the depleted St Clement Dane's School in the Strand where there 'was only the headmistress and a staff of two and the school was split into just two classes, junior from the age of five to ten ... and the seniors.' The school routine was strict ('talking was never allowed in class. If someone spoke, the whole class was made to sit with hands on heads for as long as [the teacher] chose'), and when the daytime raids started in the summer of 1940:

> it was a welcome relief when the sirens went and we could disappear down to the basement. While the raid was on we worked on small pieces of tapestry and one of the teachers would read us stories from literature – of adventure and derring-do, of exciting places and fantastic happenings. For a time it shut out immediate events around us and softened the dull crump, crump sound that shook us from time to time. By the time I was ten years old, thanks to Hitler, I had grown to love poetry and was familiar with Shakespeare's *A Midsummer Night's Dream*. ...

[But when the] Blitz in London ... began in earnest, the air-raid sirens that we

The shelterers

'"All Clear" in the morning.'
A painting by Edward
Ardizzone.

Before the war, Edward Ardizzone was best known as the author and illustrator of children's books. **Little Tim and the Brave Sea Captain** (1936), his first and most successful, was based on stories he told his own children about his childhood in Ipswich and his love of boats and the sea. He also drew for the **Radio Times**. In 1939, Ardizzone (his father was of Italian extraction) was serving in an anti-aircraft regiment when he was appointed as an official war artist and sent to France with the British Army. Rescued from Boulogne as it was bombed – a scene he painted – he was back in Britain as the Blitz began and his own home in Maida Vale, west London suffered a near miss in an air raid.

Captain Ardizzone was then commissioned (as, later, was Henry Moore) to paint the 'curious colonies' of shelterers that formed nightly in underground stations in London. Ardizzone's pictures were affectionate, showing the humour and warmth as well as the squalor in which whole families lived their lives underground for months.

While some were enthusiastic about their life underground – 'the shelterers were very, very friendly and you'd never know there was a war on down there,' said one – a journalist who visited the Elephant and Castle tube station was appalled:

> From the platform to the entrance the whole station was one incumbent mass of humanity. ... It took me a quarter of an hour to get from the station entrance to the platform. Even in the darkened booking hall I stumbled over huddled bodies, bodies which were no safer from bombs than if they had lain in the gutters of the silent streets outside. Going down the stairs I saw mothers feeding infants at the breast. Little girls and boys lay across their parents' bodies because there was no room on the winding stairs. Hundreds of men and women were partially undressed while small boys and girls slumbered in the foetid atmosphere absolutely naked. Electric lights blazed, but most of this mass of suffering humanity slept as though they were between silken sheets.

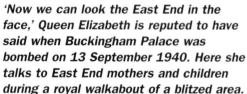

'Now we can look the East End in the face,' Queen Elizabeth is reputed to have said when Buckingham Palace was bombed on 13 September 1940. Here she talks to East End mothers and children during a royal walkabout of a blitzed area.

Above right: Children in a London air-raid shelter watch a puppet show with puppets some of them have made.

had looked forward to with so much excitement had, through repetition, lost much of their charm. There was no escape from their mournful wail. Living opposite the stamp factory had its benefits. On the first sound of the sirens nobody bothered to make for the shelters. We listened for the whistle sounded for the workers. [A system introduced so that war production would be interrupted as little as possible.] One blast meant warning; two blasts meant enemy planes overhead. On hearing three, the inhabitants of 'D' block magically appeared on the landings and hurried down to the shelter that we shared with 'E' block. If the sirens went during the hours of daylight when we kids were playing in the yard, we ignored the sirens and whistles. We became experts at listening to the sound of the ack-ack [anti-aircraft] guns and could tell exactly how far away the German planes were. We were deaf to the yells of adults telling us to come into the shelter until we heard the urgent sound of close guns and the throb of German engines.

When there was a night-time raid, however, Barbara Roose made her way down to the communal brick-built shelter and worried about her mother:

She and Geoff took shelter in the alcove beside the coal bunker. ... I was always uneasy thinking of them up there on the fourth floor especially if the bombers were directly overhead. ... Mum always came out with the old adage 'If your number's on it, you'll go.' We were lucky and nothing happened to us but I preferred to take my own chances than to be around if their number was on it.

When to shelter, where to shelter, was an essential wartime preoccupation. Local Authorities had been charged by the Air Raid Precautions Act of 1937 with responsibility for 'the protection of persons and property from attack and injury and damage in the event of hostile attacks from the air'. The government's guiding principle was dispersal. It was essential to avoid hundreds of people gathering in one place, with the high death toll that would follow should a bomb fall on it. This dictated that, on the outbreak of war, cinemas, theatres, sports meetings – anywhere where large crowds gathered – were shut down, though they were soon reopened. This policy was the main reason why the government refused either to construct large deep underground shelters, or to allow the tube stations to be used as they had in the First World War. Other important factors were cost and the fear that a 'deep shelter' mentality would develop, with 'timorous troglodytes' refusing to come up again after a raid, with the result that transport and communication would be paralysed.

Efforts were concentrated on individual shelters. People living in houses or blocks of flats with basements or cellars were encouraged to use these during raids, and it was pointed out that they could be made reasonably comfortable with mattresses, cushions and rugs, rudimentary heating and lighting. Grants were available to strengthen the building's structure if necessary. Households could also erect a government-supplied 'Anderson shelter' (named after the Home Secretary, Sir John Anderson) which were arched corrugated-iron and steel structures that were dug into the ground and provided protection for a family from blast and debris, though not from a direct hit. These structures were issued free to families with an income of less than £250 a year. On the outbreak of war, some 1.5 million Anderson shelters had been distributed free to those who lived in the 'danger areas' where bombs were expected to fall. It was optimistically supposed that these would shelter around 6 million people – but that was still not protection enough.

An Anderson shelter, however, was no use to tenement dwellers nor those living in back-to-back terraces with no gardens; these often poorly-built properties were also unlikely to have suitable cellars or basements. The solution for their occupants had to be public shelters. Some of these were requisitioned basements in public buildings such as libraries or

'Passing the Time': children playing draughts in a shelter, painted by Edmund Kapp for the official War Artists scheme in 1940.

99

100

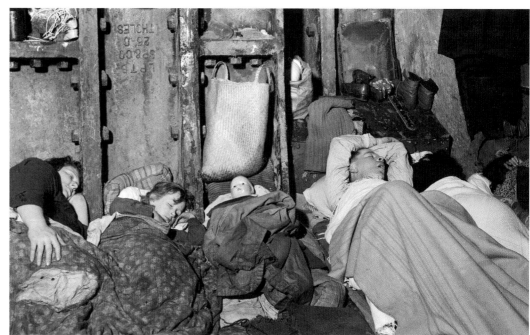

An ARP board game in which the aim was to get to the All Clear, and such 'incidents' as incendiary bombs falling, or a gas attack alert, moved a player faster round the board.

Above right: Sheltering from the Blitz. A family asleep on the platform at Liverpool Street underground station in November 1940. Even the little girl's doll has its own improvised bed.

town halls, or in commercial premises or institutions (Florence Rollinson spent many a Blitz night in the Bryant & May shelter in Bow). Others were purpose-built brick structures. They were intended for people with no individual shelter, and for those caught out by a raid in the street. Since raids were expected to be intense but short, these shelters were built without facilities such as seating or lavatories or running water. When the Blitz came and the Alert might last all night, they soon became damp, malodorous and generally unpopular, particularly when so many were tragically found to be unable to withstand nearby bomb blasts.

Early in the war, 'as if by magic a surface shelter suddenly appeared' in each of the yards that divided the tenement buildings where Barbara Roose's family lived. When the Blitz finally came, however, her mother, like many householders, preferred to huddle in the cupboards under the stairs when the siren sounded. This was also often the case with those who had an Anderson shelter, because it was so cold down there at the bottom of the garden, or the shelter was flooded (which happened frequently), or just frightening as shrapnel falling on the metal roof could sound 'like a coal scuttle being emptied' and make the bombs seem very near.

At the start of the Blitz, many East Enders bypassed government restrictions and took matters into their own hands. They sheltered where they felt safest, under bridges or railway arches, which in fact offered little protection. When the bombers came back on the second night of the Blitz, Bernard Kops recalls:

People started to flock towards the tube. They wanted to get underground. Thousands upon thousands … pushed their way into Liverpool Street station [and other underground stations] demanding to be let down to shelter. At first the authorities wouldn't hear of it and they called out the soldiers to bar the way. ... I stood there with my father and mother and brothers and sisters thinking that there would be panic and we would all be crushed to death. ... The people would not give up and would not disperse, would not take no for an answer. A great yell went up and the gates were opened and my mother threw her hands together and clutched them towards the sky. ... 'It's a great victory for the working class,' a man said. 'One of our big victories.'

Tube sheltering became a way of life for Bernard Kops, as for many London children:

> I would scoot out of the train ahead of the family and ... I bagged any space I could along the platform. The family followed and we pitched our 'tent' [of scarves], then we unravelled and unwound and relaxed. And out came the sandwiches and the forced good humour. ... Our spirits would rise for a while, we were alive for another night, we would see another dawn.

101

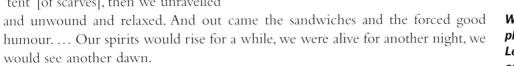

When all the space was taken on the platform of underground stations, Londoners would take shelter by sleeping on the escalators.

The young Kops managed to get some money out of his mother:

> I got bars and bars of chocolate out of the chocolate vending machines and weighed myself incessantly. Here was a new life, a whole network, a whole city under the world. We rode up and down the escalators. The children of London were adapting themselves to the times, inventing new games, playing hopscotch while their mothers suckled young babies on the concrete. And I used to ride backwards and forwards in the trains to see the other stations of underground people.

Faced with a *fait accompli*, the government reversed its policy: people would be allowed to use a number of tube stations and the odd disused branch line for shelter. Fifteen miles of platforms and tunnels were designated, and at the height of the Blitz 177,000 people sought shelter there – though that was only about 4 per cent of the population of central London and a lot fewer than the 27 per cent who took to their Anderson shelters in a

The Tilbury shelter in Commercial Road, in the East End, was the most notorious shelter in London. Here children attempt to brighten up their wartime 'dormitory' by painting murals on the walls.

raid. And the underground was no guarantee of safety. Marble Arch and Trafalgar Square were hit. When Balham station received a direct hit on 14 October 1940, 64 people died or were buried alive. At Bank station on 11 January 1941, 111 people (including 57 who had taken shelter there) were crushed by falling masonry or thrown onto the line and electrocuted.

Gradually conditions improved: lavatories were installed, bunks erected, canteens established and medical care given to parents and children, not only to deal with injuries but also to treat childhood ailments and prevent infections spreading in the often fetid atmosphere.

Recalling those days, a London woman who was six years old in 1940 wrote:

Those of us who were left in London became quite used to the routine of the early evening. For a while we sheltered in our own Anderson shelter, but then we found that our neighbours were 'going down the tube'. The children in siren-suits [one-piece garments similar to the garb Winston Churchill habitually wore] and mothers carrying whatever she thought we might need: food, blankets, comics – anything in fact. There was no rush, no panic, just a steady stream of people making for the shelter where we children would find our friends and have a noisy game before settling down for the night. The tube trains still ran, of course, and they still had to cope with passengers and I remember we had to sleep on the platforms and there was a white painted line beyond which we were not allowed to lie.

After the last train, of course, it got much better – and if we continued to go down the tube regularly (and were lucky) we could even be allocated a steel bunk. I did eventually get to sleep on one, but it wasn't very comfortable. … We were all encouraged to sing in the shelters. My sister and I entered the fancy dress competition. How they found the enthusiasm for this I just don't know.

Reginald Baker 'caught impetigo from being down the tube' when he came back to London from being evacuated.

I caught scabies, which is terrible. You had to go to the local health office and they'd paint you – like a Red Indian. … It was rampant because it was wartime and in shelters and down the tube people were sleeping all crammed up close together.

102

I was embarrassed though so I didn't go to school. And you could play truant from school for a week – two weeks – because if when you went back, the teacher asked you where you'd been you'd say 'Oh my mum kept me down the tube sir, she wouldn't let me come up.' And they couldn't argue with that because people were down the tube day and night in the East End. A lot were.

Isabel Kiernan, who lived in Liverpool, was 12 when the war started.

On 21 December we were bombed out. … We were in our usual place under the stairs. My sister and I (fully clothed as the raids became more severe, with overcoats to hand) and our dog lay on a mattress and slept when possible. My mother and father sat in the pantry, which was also under the stairs. My brother was at sea – my special hero *he* was. The raid started as usual at teatime. It was always a rush to get tea over and 'pots' cleared away before the siren went … After a dreadful night with mobile ack-ack guns going off around us and a tremendous number of bombs and incendiaries falling, we heard different explosions, which were later found to be landmines. Soon after these, all resistance from the ack-ack guns seemed to end. We could only hear bombs and the thud-thud drone of German planes. … It was bright moonlight and the first 'near miss' blew our windows in at the back of the house. The bomb didn't whine, it just sounded like a gust of wind before the explosion. My father dashed into the kitchen and could see the windows blown out and the curtains in shreds. He shouted, 'The blackout!' and threw a kettleful of water on the dying embers of the fire in the grate. There were always lulls in the raids and during one of these my father had a look out and saw the whole area seemed to be on fire and there were lots of people shouting and firemen and wardens terribly active. We stayed in our places under the stairs and soon afterwards … a bomb fell in our back garden and I must say I was scared stiff. We stayed where we were and everything seemed to be falling in on us. We were quite unharmed, but my father said we mustn't move until the bombing stopped. Water started running down the stairs and the hall became flooded, but we were not wet. At dawn when the raid was over we looked out and found the hall full of

Above: A family shelter. Mrs Shepherd of Downham Estate in Kent reads to her seven children in the double-sized Anderson shelter in the back garden.

Below: Punch, 20 December 1940.

"*You can't go in there to-day. It's too deep.*"

103

104 **Right: Danger UXB. A London child plays by a notice indicating that there is an unexploded bomb and the street has been roped off until the UXB squad can get there to remove or defuse it.**

water and our hats and coats floating about. The stairs were covered with rubble and my father went upstairs and said the water tank was leaking, and that all the beds were covered in rubble and broken glass. The front-room furniture had been thrown all over the room and the windows were blown out from a bomb which had a direct hit opposite us. The road was full of rescue workers and I saw a friend of mine carried by a blanket and the blanket was over her head and I knew she was dead.

As we were wandering around the house my brother came running home – he had sailed up the River Mersey and had seen both sides of the river on fire and wondered if we were still alive. He started looking round the house and found a large unexploded bomb in the side passage between our house and next door. ... My father reported it to the ARP men and shortly after the police came and ordered us all out. We collected a few belongings and my mother gathered some food in a basket and we left our house, walking in rubble and crunching broken glass. It was light now and the sky was red with the reflection of fires. When we

'Children Buried and Killed in an Unexploded Bomb Incident, Gurney Street, Southwark' painting by S.H. Rothwell. Iris Ward was 14 when the explosion occurred near the Elephant and Castle on 6 June 1942. 'It was just as if someone had opened a great big oven. The heat rolled, literally rolled, up the street ... I could feel something on top of me. It was either a little girl or a little boy ...' 37 people were killed when the buried UXB or mine exploded months after the last air raid.

reached the top of the hill on our way to knock up some friends and ask if we could stay a while, we looked back over the river and the whole of Liverpool seemed to be on fire. There was a sugar refinery and oil storage tanks on fire and through it all we could see the [unfinished] tower of the new Anglican cathedral safely standing.

We stayed a day at our friends' house while my father went to the Town Hall with the other 'refugees' to find out what to do. It turned out that we couldn't return to our house for any belongings until the unexploded bomb was removed, and also my father had to find somewhere for us to live, as our house was too damaged. He was very angry and ... kept blaming the German schoolboys who had been at our local schools on exchange visits before the war. ... He was certain they had taken home photographs and maps of Merseyside and the docks and shipyards. ... He had bought his house after the 'last' war and struggled to pay for it and now the 'bloody Huns' had bombed it to blazes.

It was not Liverpool's first 'night of hell'. On 28–9 November, 350 tons of high explosives, 30 huge landmines (eight of which failed to explode) and 30,000 incendiaries had blanketed the city, killing 300. At Durning Road Instructional Centre in Edge Hill, 164 people were killed – many of them children – and more were seriously injured. Joe Lucas, one of six children, was fortunate not to be there that night. He had whooping cough and had been keeping people in the shelter awake, so his mother decided to keep him and his baby sister Brenda at home with her. She sent her other four children along to the Durning Street shelter in the care of the oldest, Florence, aged 17. All four were killed.

Veronica Goddard, a schoolgirl living with her parents in London Earls Court had begun to feel that 'we'll be the only pebbles on the beach soon'. Neighbour after neighbour fled their homes as the Blitz continued, leaving the Goddard family with the keys to their various houses. Veronica used to 'make myself comfortable in the passage' when the Alert – 'Wailing Willie' as she called it – sounded. 12–13 September 1940 was:

> a terrific night. First and foremost we had a new anti-aircraft barrage which continued almost unceasingly during the night. Crack after crack, bang after bang – it went right through one. And bombs – they fell like hailstones. High explosives, incendiaries, and time bombs. There was no scarcity of any of them. Down they whistled, crash and then: 'Where was that?' Always that question. We never knew but we had a good guess: more than often we were streets out in our surmising, but no one cared.

Ronald McGill's parents tried to shelter their children from some of the traumas:

> They used to keep it from us if any of our friends were killed. ... Mum used to say, 'Oh yes, so and so's been evacuated again,' when they weren't around, and I didn't find out for several years, until I was about 14, that some of those who had been 'evacuated' had in fact been killed.

It was remarkable how well many children seemed to cope with the Blitz. Celia Fremlin worked for Mass-Observation, an organisation that during the war was used to monitor public morale and discover how people all over Britain had been affected by the war, and what they thought of how government and local authorities were dealing with wartime conditions. She conducted a survey of children in air raids over several months in 1940. Before the Blitz, Miss Fremlin had watched a group of nine-year-olds in Bethnal Green playing at 'Air Raids':

> The children's voices rose in a long, low wail ... rose, fell and rose again in unison, imitating (most realistically) the sound of the air-raid siren. As the last wail died

Children take advantage of the emergency bath service provided by the makers of Lifebuoy soap, for those who had no hot water after an air raid.

For bravery in wartime

The youngest person to be awarded the George Medal, created in September 1940 as a 'mark of honour' for men and women who showed outstanding valour on the Home Front, was Charity Bick.

Miss Bick was only 14 when she applied to join the ARP Services Despatch Riders Team. The minimum age was 16, so she lied about her age. In February 1941, during a very heavy raid on West Bromwich near Birmingham when incendiary bombs were falling all around, Charity Bick helped her father, an ARP post warden, put one out on a shop roof using a stirrup pump. The pump jammed, but nothing daunted, Charity splashed water on the burning device with her hands and eventually extinguished it. As she was climbing down from the roof, the charred rafters gave way and she fell through the room below, sustaining minor injuries.

As soon as the Bicks had got back to the ARP post, high-explosive bombs began to fall and a terrific explosion nearby knocked them to the ground. They discovered that three nearby houses had been destroyed and, as all the other wardens were on duty elsewhere and phone lines had been put out of action, Charity Bick borrowed a bicycle and rode a mile and a quarter through falling shrapnel and bombs to get a message to the Control Post about the incident. The raid was so ferocious that she had to dismount from her bike several times and take shelter, or lie flat on the ground. Covered in grime and dirt she eventually made it to the Control Post, delivered her message and made three more journeys at the height of the raid to deliver more messages.

Charity Bick was commended for her award for outstanding courage and coolness in what were described as 'very trying circumstances'.

Below: When she was old enough Charity joined the Women's Auxiliary Air Force (WAAF), in which she served for 22 years. At the end of her wartime service she had added to her George Medal (on extreme left) the Defence Medal 1939–45 and the War Medal 1939–45.

Above: Portrait of Charity Bick, GM, by Alfred Reginald Thomson, RA.

108

Ethel Gabain was commissioned as an official War Artist under the scheme run by Sir Kenneth Clark. Here she attracts the attention of two schoolboys as she records the ruins of a bombed building.

LEAVE THIS TO US SONNY — <u>YOU</u> OUGHT TO BE OUT OF LONDON

MINISTRY OF HEALTH. EVACUATION SCHEME

away, one of the little girls stepped forward in the role of 'Teacher'. 'No panic, girls, no panic please,' she commanded in beautiful mimicry of a harassed teacher. ''As anyone forgot their gas mask …? Then go 'ome and get it.' … 'Ome was a cupboard at the side of the room, and the accused children scuttled thither to collect their imaginary gas masks under a barrage of threats and exhortations from 'Teacher'. As the game continued, this cupboard became an 'air-raid shelter', in and around which they all huddled together and sang songs. … At intervals a 'whistle' blew, and they all came out again, always under heavy instruction from 'Teacher'. …This was a girls' game. Meantime, boys at the same play centre were also playing 'Air Raids' – but in a very different style.

In contrast to the relatively ordered make-believe evolved by the girls, the nine-year-old boys interpreted the theme by racing wildly up and down, knocking furniture about, bashing into one another and screaming 'Help!' at the tops of their voices. The game became so wild that it had to be forbidden, and the boys agreed to play 'Gangsters and Cops'. To the onlooker … this game appeared exactly the same as 'Air Raids'. …

Into the midst of this fantasy war arrived, at long last, the real thing. What did the kids make of *that*?

'As for kids, they sleep through everything – wonderful isn't it?' remarked a

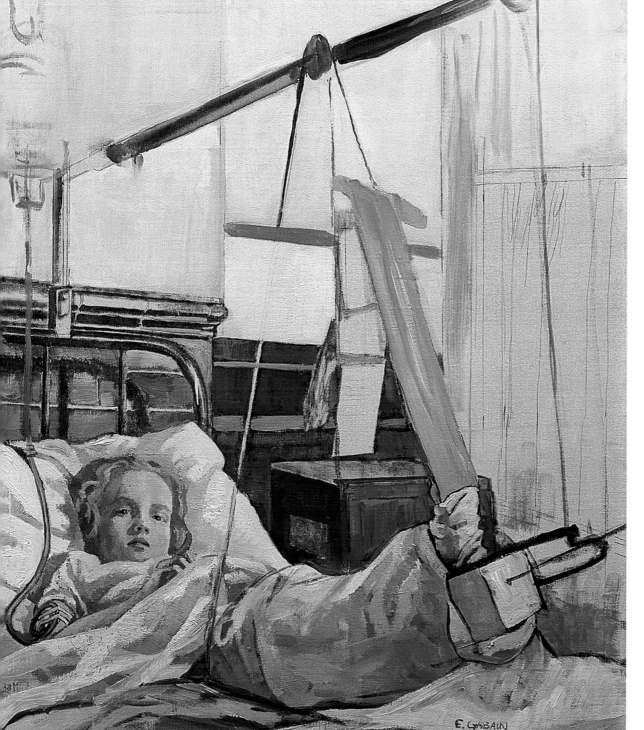

'A Child Bomb Victim Receiving Penicillin' painted by Ethel Gabain. Miss Gabain suggested to the War Artists Advisory Committee (WAAC) that Alexander Fleming, the discoverer of penicillin, would be a suitable subject for a portrait – since 'it is miraculous what penicillin has done,' she wrote to the committee. 'It has saved numberless lives on all battle fronts and everyday it is becoming more potent as a saver of life – it seems so worthy of record in all the destruction of war.'

While working on the portrait, Ethel Gabain was taken by Fleming on a tour of treatment wards and as a result, she proposed the idea of recording penicillin's clinical use to the WAAC. In 1944 she was commissioned to paint a child bomb victim in hospital. Gabain may have assumed that Gillian Samuel (pictured here) was such a victim, but in fact the child had been injured in a road accident. However, this hardly diminishes the importance of the work as evidence of the efficacy of penicillin. Gillian's leg was in danger of having to be amputated, but her mother had heard of Fleming's work and urged that she should be one of the small number of patients used to test the wonder drug.

Coventrated

The Blitz on Coventry would add an unwelcome new word to the German language: 'Coventrieren' or 'Coventrate' – to lay waste by aerial bombardment. The raid came to this thriving Midlands industrial city, where thousands of factories making car and aeroplane parts had been turned over to war production, on 14–15 November 1940. The first bombers came over at 7.20 p.m. The All Clear did not sound unto 6 o'clock the next morning. A 14-year old girl and her parents, 'ankle-deep in glass made our slow way … [out of the shelter] and had our first glimpse of Coventry, absolutely flattened.' All that was left of the Cathedral was the spire; a twelfth of all the dwellings in a city that already had an acute housing shortage were now destroyed or uninhabitable, and two-thirds of the remainder had been damaged. A young mother whose windows and doors had been blown out heard a child in the street crying, 'Mummy, where is our house?'

Almost everyone in the city knew someone who had been killed or injured, or was missing. There were 568 dead and 1,200 injured, and the figure would have been even higher had not earlier raids driven people to trek out of the city into the countryside.

Coventry was one of the first places in Britain during the Second World War to hold mass funerals and bury many of its dead in a communal grave. A school child whose two young cousins had been killed in the raid asked, 'as we looked down on the coffins one on top of another in the communal grave, "Which is Muriel and David?" No one knew.'

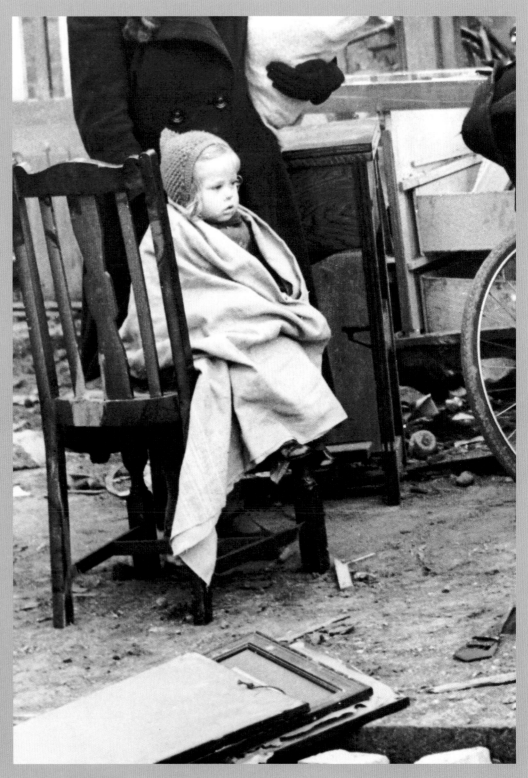

delivery man in Maida Vale during the second week of the Blitz and on September 15th in Lewisham. …The children seemed in high spirits. In an air-raid shelter some were playing 'He'. They stopped and a little boy said to another 'What's it like to be bombed?' 'Well, it's not very nice to have bricks fall on you,' replied the second, and went on with the game. It transpired that the second boy had been in a house that had received a direct hit.

Similar evidence of the relative toughness of young children was found in the Isle of Dogs [in east London's dockland], which was visited … on September 12th, after three nights of heavy and continuous bombing.

One on-the-spot report records that:

Swansea families take refuge in one of the city's rest centres. After the South Wales port was heavily bombed for three successive nights in February 1941, 14 rest centres were opened to accommodate more than 2,000 people. In addition between 2,000 and 3,000 people were estimated to be trekking out of Swansea every night to Mumbles and the Gower Peninsula to escape the bombs.

112

Mothers and children in a working-class area of Swansea, badly hit in the February 1941 raids, queue up for tea and sandwiches from a mobile canteen.

Children in particular seem to be bearing up well, and show no signs of sleeplessness or anxiety. ... Some were playing in the road near some ruins, others were walking in the street. ... One little boy was proudly showing an ARP man where his home had been – the top floor of a block of flats which had received a direct hit – while in Stepney after [a raid] an excited seven-year-old emerged from the basement of his shattered home: 'I 'ad me socks and shoes on *in bed*!' he announced: this to him had been the big drama of the occasion. And in a Bermondsey rest centre for the bombed-out, a woman helper, asking a six-year-old where her mum was, received the answer: 'Dad's been and gone and got blowed up, and Mum has gone to look for 'is bits.'

Trekkers

'Nothing I had seen prepared me for the sight of Plymouth,' wrote the US correspondent Quentin Reynolds, who had seen plenty of blitzed and devastated cities during his wartime tour of duty in Europe. In March, April and May 1941, raids devastated the city as night after night the bombers came back, and 932 people were killed – 72 when a bomb hit a public shelter in Portland Square. In addition 40,000 people had been made homeless in a city that had been designated 'safe' when evacuation plans had been drawn up back in 1939. Now the homeless and the fearful fled, heaping their possessions into cars in the unlikely event that they possessed one, or onto bicycles, prams and pushchairs, or just picked up all they could carry and headed out, as far away as possible from the harbour and docks that were the bombers' target. On 24 April, as many as 50,000 people trudged wearily out of Plymouth to find what shelter they could for themselves and their families in the surrounding woods and fields. 'Defeatists' some dared to call the nightly trekkers; with inadequate shelters, homes destroyed and social services that were past breaking point, most would surely have called the trekkers rational beings.

The seven-year-old daughter of a 'professional Hampstead man' was reported to be 'more excited than frightened nowadays and particularly likes the unusual amount of adult attention she gets. She asks all the time how a shell works, how a bomb works.'

A primary schoolteacher in Sheffield reported after a major attack on the city:

> The children referred very little to the night's raid. My train was late, so my class greeted me with: 'I thought you'd been bombed!' – evidently a huge joke … and then seemed glad to settle down to normal routine. … The children from damaged homes had just the same attitude of cheerful acceptance.

The report concluded that:

> Observations of children all over London throughout the Blitz tended to confirm the initial impression of all-round toughness and resilience in the face of bombing. In all the shelters, in the streets, and in their homes they continued to play, to squabble and to dawdle time away as much as they had done in peacetime, the only notable difference being that the age-old games of pursuit and capture now had different names: 'Cops and Robbers' was replaced by 'Convoy' or by 'Rescue Party' – a game in which the seekers hunt out the hiders as of old, but instead of 'capturing' them, they 'rescue' them, i.e. tie them up with clothes line and drag them away, just as in the good old days.

The magazine *Housewife* offered the common sense advice that, for younger children, air raids:

> 'will only mean a great noise, and provided Daddy and Mummy don't mind, *they* won't. But it is no good pretending to older children that raids are of no importance. Far better to reassure them by admitting the danger, but stressing the very long odds against being hit. … Also explain that the slightly shaky, sick feeling which they experience during raids is not really being afraid but is the result of the interference with normal vibrations in the atmosphere due to the explosion.
>
> This will help take away that feeling of guilt that schoolboys and even schoolgirls are apt to experience when they fear they are not being as brave as they would like to be. …
>
> But … even sleeping children must never be left alone during a raid.

Getting the children away. A bulldog joins children at play in an American Jewish funded nursery set up in the countryside for children affected by the Blitz.

It is true that many will become accustomed to sleep through the most terrific noise, but an extra loud explosion may wake them – and they will find much comfort in a sleepy, indifferent murmur from a trusted "grown-up" saying that it is only a fight and that the English are winning.'

This robust approach drew some reinforcement from the work of Anna Freud, daughter of the founder of psychoanalysis, Sigmund Freud, and herself a respected psychoanalyst, who had fled to London with her father from Nazi-occupied Vienna in 1938. She set up residential nurseries with her friend and colleague, Dorothy Burlingham, where they could both help and observe children who had been affected by evacuation or the Blitz, or often both.

It can be safely said that all the children who were over two years old at the time of the London Blitz have acquired knowledge of the significance of air raids. They recognise the sound of flying aeroplanes … [and] distinguish vaguely between the sound of falling bombs and anti-aircraft guns. They realise that houses will fall down when bombed and that people are often killed or hurt in falling houses. They know that fires can be started by incendiaries and that roads are often blocked as a result of bombing. They fully understand the significance of taking shelter. … Though here in England [children] are spared the actual horror of seeing people fight around them, they are not spared sights of destruction, death and injury from air raids. … It is this situation which led many people to expect that children would receive traumatic shock from air raids and would develop abnormal reactions very similar to the traumatic or war neurosis of soldiers in the last war.

However, Freud and Burlingham concluded:

On the basis of our own case material, which excludes children who have received severe bodily injuries in air raids … though it does not exclude children who have been bombed repeatedly and partly buried by debris. So far as we can notice there were no signs of traumatic shock to be observed in these children. If these bombing incidents occur when small children are in the care either of their own mothers or a familiar mother substitute they do not seem to be particularly affected by them. … This is borne out by … nurses or social workers in London County Council Rest Centres where children used to arrive in the middle of the night, straight from their bombed houses. They also found that children who arrived with their own families showed little excitement and no undue disturbance. They slept and ate normally

Children who were deemed to be suffering physically or mentally from the effects of the air raids could be legally compelled to leave London. These under-fives, the first to leave London under the new legislation, are bathed at an LCC residential school near Windsor.

115

and played with whatever toys they had rescued or which might be provided. It is a widely different matter when children during an experience of this kind are separated from or even lose their parents.

Peter Holloway was back in Bermondsey from his de luxe evacuation when the Blitz started, and in early October:

We received an incendiary through the roof which grandpa put out with a stirrup pump and sand. The roof was badly damaged and we had no windows left in the house. The windows were boarded up and the doors locked. A canvas sheet was put over the damaged part of the roof and some workmen put timber beams from the front walls down to the middle of the road where they met another beam serving the same purpose for the house opposite. We took cases with as many of our belongings as we could carry and slung our gas masks over our shoulders through the shambles of broken glass and masonry. ... The bus took us to the Elephant and Castle Underground station where we joined hundreds of other refugees in transit. We were given blankets and a place to sleep on the platform and we were told that the bombs couldn't reach us there. I lay awake all night listening for the bombs – and it was true – they couldn't get you down there in the Underground. Hot soup and bread were provided as people came and went. ...

After three days we left the Underground and went by bus to a house which I believe had been requisitioned by the London County Council in Morden [Surrey]. It was thought to be a temporary shelter before evacuation, but it was still a dangerous part of London. ... Although the air raids were just as frequent, they did not seem so frightening. Yet it was about this time that I developed a nervous illness known as 'bomb shock'. I would start to shake uncontrollably, not necessarily during an air raid. I was deeply ashamed of this but there was nothing I could do about it.

Towards the end of October ... we took to the Anderson shelter during a night raid. It was less frightening than many I had experienced before in dockland, but a string of heavy bombs took out the whole of our side of the street, blasting the building on top of the shelter. I have no recollection of the explosions and only remember the ARP clearing the rubble from the shelter during the morning to get us out. My mother said later that I was blown from one side of the Anderson onto my brother's bunk opposite, but I recall nothing of that. ... We were taken to an ARP post with our suitcase belongings. My mother had taken them into the shelter with us – just in case. My prize possession at that time was an antique soft toy given to me by my maternal grandmother, who had kept it since childhood. It was a penguin with one eye and a flipper missing. My mother made a new flipper from a piece of old handbag and stitched on an embroidered eye. This was my constant companion and I made certain it came with me to the shelter for its own safety. It rejoiced in the name of Woofy and must have been at least 70 years old.

Left: London children who had been made homeless by air raids are entertained at the Hertfordshire home of the blunt Yorkshire playwright and novelist J.B. Priestley, where they had been offered a refuge.

A letter from the Lord Mayor of Portsmouth sent at Christmas 1940 to all children who had been evacuated from the city.

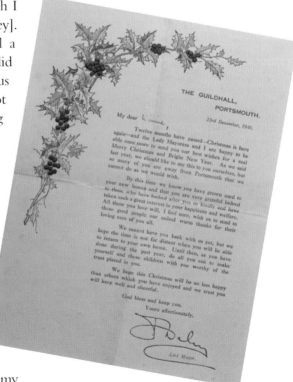

We arrived at the ARP station and joined others who had also been bombed out. Some had been less fortunate than us and ambulance men were dealing with the casualties from the bombing. Sometime towards the late afternoon we were taken by bus to a new temporary home in Raynes Park in a quieter part of London to await evacuation to the country though we had no idea where. That night my father appeared as if by magic and after earnest discussion which was incomprehensible to me, my parents made arrangements for us to join a party of evacuees to Waterloo. We were given a number and a group to join but no fixed destination. Our train was due to depart later that week, but we had to go to Waterloo in readiness for immediate departure should it be necessary. A few days later we were crammed into a compartment and locked in to avoid any possibility of children trying to leave the train. A Mrs Catasides was put in charge of about 15 children. She was a huge lady and wore an extraordinary blue hat, the kind that ladies wear at Ascot. She had a large loaf of bread and bread knife, but no butter or jam. We stared miserably out of the window at our parents as the train slowly steamed out of the station on a foggy November morning. I clung on to Woofy and Stanley [Peter's older brother] clung on to me as the train gathered speed. We did not cry, we all sat in total silence as the last air-raid warning we were to hear sounded out over London.

118

Painting by Ruskin Spear, 1942.

5

Cogs in the war machine

The leaflet shown reads:

Your Children's **FOOD IN WARTIME**

MINISTRY OF FOOD — WAR COOKERY LEAFLET 10 — Number 9

You want your children to be healthy and happy, of course and to grow up strong and sturdy. Do you know that all that depends very largely upon the food you give them now, and the food habits you help them to form? By following the few simple rules given in this leaflet, you can do much to make sure that your children build sound constitutions and healthy, active bodies.

Why is a child's food so vitally important?

1. Because a child develops bones, muscles and teeth entirely from food. Through the mother before birth, and in the diet of early and late childhood.
2. A child's food must also provide for the daily upkeep of the body, for protection against illness and for the supply of energy for almost ceaseless activity.
3. The younger the child, the smaller the quantity of food that can be taken at one meal; therefore each food served must be of good nutritional value.

Foods that build bones, muscle and teeth

1 MILK

A. Take full advantage of the Government's Milk Schemes. See that your child gets all the "priority" milk he or she is entitled to at home, and that school children get milk in school wherever possible.

B. See that each child in the family actually consumes his or her full allowance of milk, and that it is not given to any grown-up.

C. Use the National Household Skimmed Milk as an extra when it is obtainable.

D. Use milk in vegetable soups and stews, as well as in puddings, sauces and drinks.

'War's a nuisance,' pronounced ten-year-old Gerald in a magazine report on 'What Children Think of the War'. 'You can't get sweets, everything's on coupons.' Food was rationed; much was unobtainable and what was available was dull and getting duller as the years of war rolled on. While no one need starve, most people felt rather hungry much of the time. In these circumstances, the needs of babies and small children were much in the forefront of official minds. A Ministry of Food announcement in early 1942 insisted:

> Priority! Children are continuously building – building bones, teeth, tissue, nerves and muscles. They draw the building from the food they eat. If the food is unsuitable, or lacking in quantity, their development is spoiled. It may be very difficult to make it up in after life, no matter how good their food may be. Therefore, where there are wartime shortages, 'fair shares for everyone' means that for certain foods children must come first.

Rationing had come into effect on 8 January 1940. Its purpose was to make sure that everyone in the country had a fair share of essential food, and to stop 'hoarding' by those who could afford to bulk buy. The first foods to 'go on the ration' were butter (4 oz per person per week), sugar (12 oz), bacon and ham (4 oz). Meat was rationed from 11 March 1940 to the value of 1/10d per person per week, so that a housewife could choose to buy a small amount of an expensive cut such as a steak or chops, or a larger amount of cheaper meat for stewing or braising. Gradually more comestibles – jam, marmalade, treacle, tea, cheese, cooking fats – were rationed, and the allowances fluctuated throughout the war. Sugar fell to 8 oz in 1940 and cheese to 1 oz in May 1942: it rose to 8 oz in July 1942 but fell back again to 3 oz in May 1943.

Those things which could not be rationed because their supply fluctuated somewhat according to the season – milk and eggs, for example – were 'allocated' rather than strictly rationed. The general expectation – though often confounded – was of rather less than one egg per person per week, and the milk allocation was progressively cut until at the end of March 1942 the entitlement was three pints per person per week. Offal was not rationed, nor were fish, fruit and vegetables – or bread until *after* the war.

Just because something was not rationed, however, it did not mean that it was in plentiful supply. Rather the reverse was the case. The government declined all attempts to ration such things as canned and processed food or dried fruit because demand and availability varied and a steady supply could not be guaranteed – which was a key requirement of the rationing system. At the beginning of December 1941 a 'points'

Daily life in wartime. Evelyn Dunbar's painting of 'The Queue at the Fish Shop'.

system was introduced. At first it covered just tinned meat, tinned fish and tinned beans, but it proved so popular that it was soon extended to cover other things. In addition to their coupons everyone received a certain number of 'points' (usually around 24), which they could spend as they liked on whatever was available. The points system gave a bit of variety to the wartime diet and introduced some small element of choice into a heavily regulated wartime life.

121

A refinement of the scheme was the 'personal points' system introduced in July 1942, which covered sweets and chocolates. The idea was that since 'little Willie would wish to make his own selection at the shop, yet little Willie could not be trusted with the vital main ration book', these points were detachable from the main ration book and were intended as an individual ration rather than going into the household pot like the other foodstuffs. Everyone over six months of age was allowed 8 oz of chocolate and confectionary every month; the ration went up to 16 oz, and finally settled at 12 oz for the remainder of the war – indeed until 1953.

Wartime chocolate was much coarser and more powdery than it had been in peacetime, and the shortage of milk meant that much more – including Kit Kat – was now produced in a plain chocolate variety. Small 'ration-sized' bars of chocolate went on sale, often wrapped in greaseproof paper since tinfoil was needed for military purposes. Zoning regulations restricted the distribution of goods to an area close to where they were produced in order to save on transport costs. This meant that any child living near Slough, for example, would be able to get Mars bars, which would probably be unobtainable further afield. Michael Foreman, who would grow up to be a writer and illustrator of children's books, took the choice at the village shop in his Suffolk village very seriously:

Pear drops, humbugs, fruit drops, liquorice comforts, gob-stoppers. You got more pear drops for your penny. But you might have to share them with your little brother or sister. … Gob-stoppers last longer and you were less likely to have to share (though

Priority children. Oranges, an important source of vitamin C in wartime, were first reserved for children when they were available.

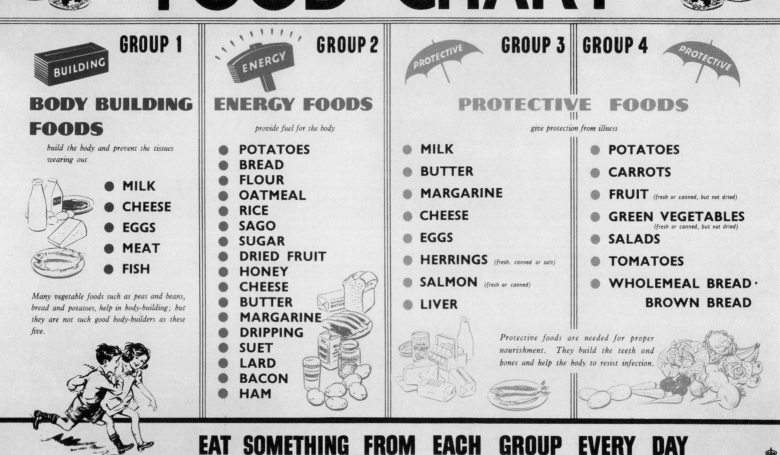

FOOD CHART

GROUP 1	GROUP 2	GROUP 3	GROUP 4
BUILDING	**ENERGY**	**PROTECTIVE**	**PROTECTIVE**
BODY BUILDING FOODS	**ENERGY FOODS**	**PROTECTIVE FOODS**	
build the body and prevent the tissues wearing out	*provide fuel for the body*	*give protection from illness*	
• MILK	• POTATOES	• MILK	• POTATOES
• CHEESE	• BREAD	• BUTTER	• CARROTS
• EGGS	• FLOUR	• MARGARINE	• FRUIT *(fresh or canned, but not dried)*
• MEAT	• OATMEAL	• CHEESE	• GREEN VEGETABLES *(fresh or canned, but not dried)*
• FISH	• RICE	• EGGS	• SALADS
	• SAGO	• HERRINGS *(fresh, canned or salt)*	• TOMATOES
	• SUGAR	• SALMON *(fresh or canned)*	• WHOLEMEAL BREAD · BROWN BREAD
	• DRIED FRUIT	• LIVER	
	• HONEY		
	• CHEESE		
	• BUTTER		
	• MARGARINE		
	• DRIPPING		
	• SUET		
	• LARD		
	• BACON		
	• HAM		

Many vegetable foods such as peas and beans, bread and potatoes, help in body-building; but they are not such good body-builders as these five.

Protective foods are needed for proper nourishment. They build the teeth and bones and help the body to resist infection.

EAT SOMETHING FROM EACH GROUP EVERY DAY

ISSUED BY THE MINISTRY OF FOOD

half-sucked gob-stoppers were often passed round, usually from my pocket and then from mouth to mouth…). Liquorice comforts were the most fun. They were sucked slowly until only the black centre remained. This stained all your teeth black. If you were careful you could blacken only a few, or every other one. Earlier in the sucking stage, while there was still colour on the comforts, you could war-paint yourself and several other members of the gang in the full range of candy colours.

An imposition which mothers found particularly irritating, but which most children probably felt pretty insouciant about, was soap rationing. This was introduced with no prior warning on 9 February 1942, and was rather offputtingly administered by the Ministry of Food because soap and margarine were both based on the same raw materials. Everybody was allowed four coupons for each four-week period, and each coupon could be used for toilet soap, hard soap (for washing clothes), soap powder or flakes. The outcry about soap rationing (or 'a little public feeling about the inadequacy'

The ration book for Princess Elizabeth, the present Queen. Whether the royal family strictly adhered to the same rations in wartime as their subjects is debatable. Produce from the royal farms supplemented the royal diet, and monogrammed pats of butter appeared on the royal table, though margarine was widely used too.

as a government history of rationing had it) led to a concession. Double soap rations were allowed for babies, since in the days long before disposal nappies had been thought of (and anyway could not have been produced in wartime due to the acute paper shortage) a great deal of washing necessarily went on if there was a baby in the house.

Children under six (later reduced to five) had a green ration book of their own – though of course it would be in the custody of their mother – and there was an extra allowance for pregnant and nursing mothers. From 1943 onwards a blue book was issued to children in the 5–16 age group (extended to 18 in 1944). Children received the same rations as adults, except that those under five were entitled to only half the meat ration and no tea. Those between 18 months and six years were allowed three eggs a week (while adults were lucky to get one) and received approximately double the allowance of dried eggs when these were introduced. Probably the most important concession was milk. The 'Radio Doctor' Charles Hill explained the system on the popular *Kitchen Front* programme that was broadcast on the Home Service every day, after the 8 a.m. news and before housewives set out to do their shopping. 'The priority groups, the mothers and young children under five, are guaranteed their [daily] pint cheap, or if necessary for nothing,' while those between five and 18 got three and a half pints on the assumption that they were getting milk daily at school. 'Health can be bought in a bottle,' proselytised Dr Hill. 'An apple a day will keep no doctors away; but a pint of milk will, if it's given to children.'

When oranges were available, they were reserved for children under 18, with double for children under five.

A small child finds difficulty in taking enough potatoes, green vegetables and salads to provide all the Vitamin C he requires. It is a matter of 'tummy capacity'. So when there are oranges to be had, it is fair that the little ones should have first call on them rather than their elders who can, and should, eat plenty of the ordinary Vitamin C foods.

After 1942, expectant or nursing mothers and children under five were entitled to subsidised orange juice (which replaced an earlier issue of blackcurrant syrup or purée when it was imported under the US Lend–Lease scheme) and cod liver oil, and could get these supplements free if they were on a low income. There was, of course, no guarantee that mothers would take up their child's entitlement. It was reckoned that probably only around 38 per cent of mothers gave their children cod liver oil when it was introduced and only 54 per cent orange juice, and this figure had not significantly risen by the end of the war. But the measure put the welfare of the next generation in the front line of wartime welfare policy – a policy that would continue into the peace.

A London child, sent to live with his aunt in Chipstead, Surrey, during the war, agonises over the choice of his monthly ration of sweets in a local shop.

Before the war, school meals had been stigmatised as being only for the poor, but evacuation and rationing changed that attitude. By 1945 the proportion of children having school dinners had risen to around 40 per cent of children in England and Wales, compared with only 4 per cent previously. Far more children were also taking advantage of free school milk. Indeed during the war, children from northern industrial cities, who had often been undernourished in the 1930s, were consuming as much milk as children from much better-off families. As a post-war Labour Party publication trumpeted, 'in spite of shortages, the children are rosy-cheeked, well-clothed. … They are taller, heavier and healthier than before the war.'

'Today we are interested in food as never before,' reported the 'Radio Doctor'. 'It's taken a war to make us interested.' This interest was no idle gourmandising: everyone recognised that food was a fuel of war and a scarce resource. The Ministry of

126

'You can use every bit of a pig except its squeal' was a popular wartime slogan, and by 1942 there were some 42,000 pig clubs throughout the country fattening up porkers for their members to consume. Children played their part in tipping household scraps into the pig bins set up on many street corners.

Food produced leaflets and took out advertisements in newspapers and magazines, advising on how to make the most of what was available and how to try to avoid the monotonous meals that such a limited range of food was likely to produce. 'Careful planning is needed to prepare suitable meals for children and food shortages call for extra effort if children are to be adequately fed,' lectured a Ministry of Food leaflet *How to Feed Young Children*. It set out a typical day's balanced diet, starting with porridge (lentil porridge was recommended by one cookbook for feeding a child in wartime) for breakfast and ending the day with a slice of bread and dripping or 'finely grated or chopped vegetables such as tomatoes, parsley, watercress and carrots (or 'finely shredded raw Brussels sprouts') made into sandwiches.' The advice concluded sagely, 'if you serve a dish to a child you don't like yourself [such as the recommended 'creamed liver' perhaps?] don't show your distaste to the child. Children like to copy their parents.'

But it wasn't only a question of being creative with what was available (in those

Babies parked while mothers shop. Fruit and vegetables were not rationed, but were often in short supply. Imported fruit was usually scarce and prohibitively expensive, but children got priority call on any oranges that were available.

moments mothers managed to fit in between endless queuing, making do and mending, and most likely doing part-time war work too). It was essential to increase food production, and this was something children were encouraged to help with too.

In the 1930s British farms had increasingly been turned over to pasture, and many of the allotments that had been so productive in the First World War were left fallow. As a predominantly urban and industrial country, Britain was a net importer of food: in peacetime some 70 per cent of cheese and sugar, nearly 80 per cent of fruit, 90 per cent of cereals and fats, and around 50 per cent of all meat came from abroad, and Britain's livestock was almost entirely dependent on imported foodstuffs. But ships in wartime were both at risk from enemy action and required to carry essential war matériel; Britain had to be much more self-sufficient in its food production.

A massive government campaign was launched to get the countryside under the plough: the target was 1.7 million more acres producing food by harvest time 1940. There

DIG FOR VICTORY

For their sake-
GROW YOUR OWN
VEGETABLES

Below: A bureaucrat's war. A photograph from a series taken for the Ministry of Information showing two children with their family's identity cards and ration books, an example of how a 'British working-class family in wartime' coped with its extraordinary conditions.

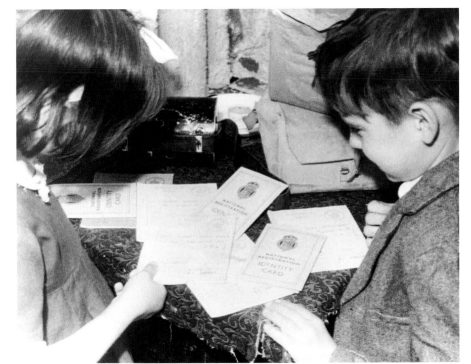

were subsidies and incentives – but there was also an acute shortage of agricultural labour as younger farm workers went into the forces – or to work in war industries to try to better their meagre agricultural wages. By 1939 there was a shortfall of over 50,000 farm workers. The founding of the Women's Land Army helped around the farm – and so too did the recruitment of young people. Local children and evacuees, who often had only half-day schooling, were recruited to help with the harvest, pick fruit, pull up potatoes and root vegetables, and any other tasks the farmers needed done. A Youth Land Army scheme was canvassed in the press, by which schoolboys would spend two or three weeks of their summer holidays living on a farm and helping with the harvest. The West of England Volunteer Harvesters Association, made up of about 130 public and secondary schools, undertook to assign boys to farms where their labour was most needed.

Farm work would not only help the farmer: it could assuage homesickness, accustom the evacuee to country ways – and use up the excess energy that might otherwise be employed less productively. An article in *Farmers Weekly* advised its readers 'to let your evacuee guests join in the work. Nothing will so satisfactorily turn their minds away from tiredness and anxiety.' At a school in north Devon:

[The children take] a very active part in the management of goats, and under the supervision of a grown-up person they do the milking, grooming, feeding and cleaning out stables. The milk is carefully recorded … and simple accounts are kept to show the profit and loss on the herd.

Other evacuees were taught to milk cows, churn butter, feed hens and collect the eggs. In August 1944, pupils from Mary Datchelor School who were over 14:

worked in Harvest Camps in two Wiltshire villages. …They had a splendid time, and won the approval of the farmers and market gardeners for whom they worked, one of whom modified his critical attitude towards girl land-workers after three of our girls had cleared in two days an onion field which would have taken his men a week.

A Liverpool child became a blacksmith's right hand man, and another child got part-time work plucking chickens. It was reported that some evacuees so enjoyed the work they did on the farms that when it was time for them to return to the cities, they opted to stay on and train for a career in agriculture. The juvenile employment authorities in Liverpool, where unemployment levels had been high in the 1930s, noted approvingly that:

Slowly, and almost solely as a natural development of the evacuation scheme, boys are beginning to see that when they reach school-leaving age, work on a farm will help the country fight its war as well as furnishing them with healthy, interesting employment.

In the autumn of 1940 it was reported that two Liverpool girls of school-leaving age had taken up agricultural work and no doubt there were several more who went 'Back to the Land', as the government slogan had it, for good.

There were other ways that country children and their wartime visitors could help the war effort. 'Why not take the children and go a-harvesting?' a Ministry of Food advertisement urged, suggesting that elderberries, sloes, crab apples, nuts and mushrooms would all enliven a wartime diet – though cautioning ' be sure that in their excitement the [children] do not damage bushes or hedges, or walk through growing crops.' A Liverpool teacher took her school into the fields most afternoons in the early autumn to pick rosehips, which earned the children 2d a pound since they could be used to make rosehip syrup, a valuable source of vitamin C when oranges were scarce. Cubs and Brownies did likewise, and in 1943 alone 500 tons of rosehips were picked – mostly by children. Other children collected ferns, foxgloves and nettles, which were despatched to Bangor University where they were used in the manufacture of dyes and medication. Extracts of horse chestnuts were used in making glucose, and the waste was experimented with as a possible animal feedstuff. The woods round Betws-y-Coed were festooned with sphagnum moss, which children carefully collected so it could be dried and used to supplement cotton wool as a dressing for wounds. Older children might help catch rabbits in the countryside, or feed them in the garden at home – and then balk at eating their pets – and collect kitchen scraps to feed the neighbourhood Pig Club's porker.

But it wasn't only nature's bounty that was culled for the war effort, nor just the farmers who would produce Britain's food. Everyone was encouraged to 'Dig for Victory', including the children. Every available piece of earth in gardens, allotments, parks, recreation grounds, railway embankments and bomb sites was to be turned over to growing vegetables – and children could help dig, sow, hoe, plant and weed. A number of schools turned parts of their playing fields into allotments, and tending them and cooking the produce became a regular part of the school curriculum. At a Brighton school the children were given the option of doing sport or working on the allotments, and many children would be roped in to help their father (or mother) tend the family allotment after school or at weekends. And all children were encouraged to collect

Below: 'Dig for Victory' in practice. Lelia Faithful's painting of 'Evacuees Growing Cabbages'.

129

Wartime babies

The magazine Housewife was concerned about babies in wartime. In the summer of 1940, an article observed that 'the babies who are being born now, or who are going to be born in the next few months, are certainly arriving at an exciting time in the world's history.' However, it was suggested that women should avoid giving birth 'in one of the more isolated coastal villages, since they rather invite invasion'.

Maybe 'exciting' wasn't quite the word most new mothers would have used as the bombs began to fall. But Housewife was on hand with practical advice.

Plan the whole of baby's outfit with the possibility of having to journey with him hastily from one place to another [presumably from home to shelter]. A Moses basket will act as a cradle and a store for napkins; a large rubber beach bag or waterproof rucksack will hold wet napkins till they can be washed. ... I would advise you to accustom baby to taking a little bottle feed after his 2.00 p.m. breast feed. ...

The point is that, however courageous you are, the actual noise of an air raid is apt to be very upsetting, and you may find yourself without milk for a few hours; then baby can have a full feed of the dried or evaporated milk to which he had become accustomed ... until when, with returning serenity, your milk comes back.

It would be a wise precaution [for those about to give birth] to have all your own requirements ... fitted into a large suitcase, so that if your own house, for any reason, [like bombing presumably] becomes uninhabitable, you can slip over the way and have your baby in the house of some hospitable friend. You'll be surprised and gratified to find how completely a confinement takes your mind off 'enemy operations'.

Two years later Mass-Observation decided to find out what people now thought about having a baby in wartime. Among men, 48 per cent considered that it was a thoroughly bad idea, whereas 52 per cent of women were in favour of the idea – in the circumstances.

Those who were opposed to the idea of bringing a new baby into a world at war were concerned that it would be a bad start in life for the child, and unfair on the mother. They stressed practical difficulties over such things as feeding and clothing a baby, and the possible psychological effects on a child of the anxieties and insecurities that parents were bound to feel in wartime. And most expressed confidence that 'the gap [in the family] can be made up in peacetime.'

Those in favour took the opposite view, believing that 'if you wait for favourable times, you'll wait for ever.' Many thought 'children provide a link with husbands who may be killed in war' and that 'a child is a pledge of faith in the future. It would be defeatist not to have them,' while other women admitted that their reasons were 'selfish ones. ... I should like to have another baby because I want to have another baby. This is a deep instinctive urge, and I don't know a single rational reason in its favour.'

In 1941 the birth rate dropped to the lowest point since records had begun, 696,000, but thereafter it rose steadily reaching a peak at 878,000 in 1944.

130

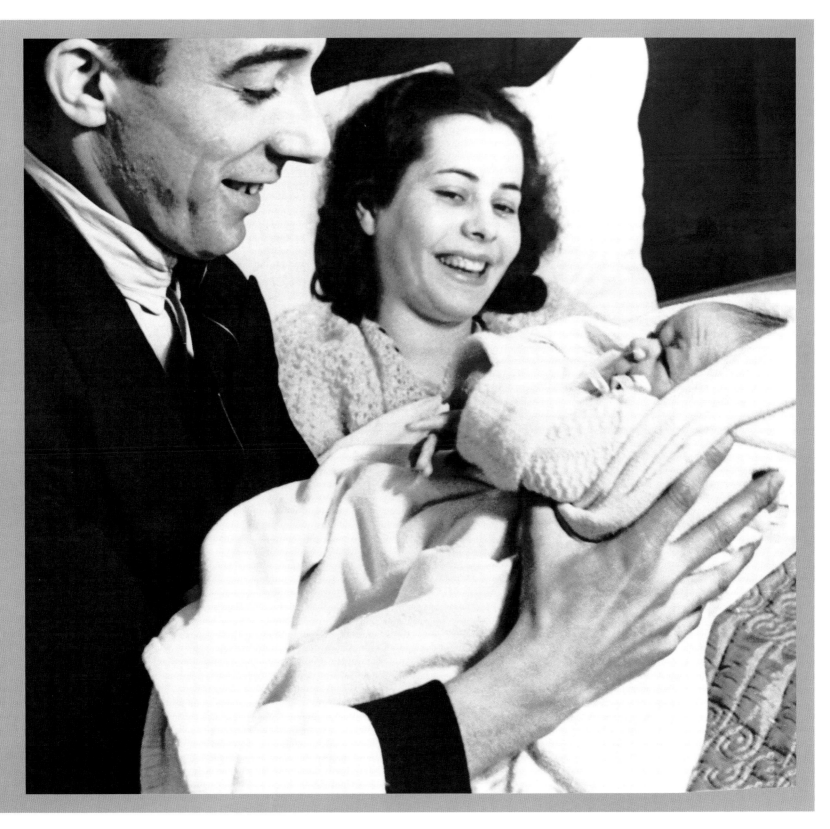

that enemy of the cabbage and Brussels sprout grower, the cabbage white butterfly, which 'caused much damage' to valuable wartime vegetable crops; some might be so lucky as to be rewarded at the rate of a penny-halfpenny per cabbage white trapped in a jam jar.

★ ★ ★

Waste paper isn't rubbish. It's precious … your waste paper is urgently needed – it's got a big job to do. … Remember that one newspaper makes three 25-pounder shell cups … six books one mortar shell carrier … one soap powder canister four aero engine gaskets … one envelope one cartridge wad. … So you see We must GO TO IT!!

So urged the Ministry of Supply advertisements, and no one 'went to it' with more alacrity than the women and children of Britain. Housewives were encouraged to be assiduous recyclers, sorting out every scrap of rubbish: paper, packaging, bones, rags, jam jars, cotton reels, string, scraps of material and wool ('a six-inch length of wool from every home in Britain' could be 'used to make 600 sets of battle dress'), and vegetable waste for pigswill. Pretty well everything could be reused, and by 1943 it was reckoned that each household in the country had produced around half a ton of salvage.

'There are not many things that small boys can do,' an article in *The Times* pointed out in 1941, 'but this is one' – the 'Cog Scheme'. The scheme was based on need and 'on the knowledge that all children like responsible, worthwhile work to do. Schools were asked to co-operate and most did.' Although most 'Cogs' were enrolled as salvage collectors through their schools, some went about their task without any adult supervision; one south London group consisted of Cogs ranging from three to 14. Leaflets and advertisements were directed at Cogs, who were instructed in 'what a Cog should know about waste paper and rags – clean ones can be remade into Admiralty charts, army blankets and battle-dress'; household bones – 'all bones are wanted except fish bones'; and metals – 'if we did not have metal scrap in this country we should have to fetch more metal from abroad, and risk seamen's lives in fetching it'. Cogs were expected to 'learn these facts by heart and teach them to others'; they were awarded badges and even had their own 'Cog Song' written by a WVS member, the opening line of which was 'There'll always be a dustbin …', which somewhat predictably

Left: 'Dig for Victory' in practice. Members of a Bethnal Green Boys' Club dig the soil to make an allotment on a bomb site in the East End.

Back to the land. Evacuees from St George's Church of England School, Battersea, help local farmers in Pembrokeshire with their haymaking at harvest time.

133

Right: 'Evacuated schoolchildren learn rural pursuits.' These London girls, evacuated to Sussex, receive instruction on how to 'look after rabbits and cure their skins.'

Below: Evacuees learn to milk a goat at Baldock in Hertfordshire.

134

was sung to the tune of 'There'll Always Be an England'.

The journalist Alice Hooper Beck reported that:

[Battersea] is full of Cogs … and I met 600 of them. The Battersea children collect everything from bits of old mangle to wooden cotton reels. Each child is responsible for the condition of the salvage he or she brings in. Paper is sorted into the correct groups and tied up in packets. Tins are crushed flat and packed into bigger tins. Bottles and jars are sorted by size. … Some of the cotton reels go back to the manufacturers to be rewound with thread and silk. Others go to the Army for the Signal Corps. … A good market has been found for used torch batteries … and now every Battersea Cog is looking for them. … Naturally [Cogs] outdo dustmen and Borough authorities in zest. Collections have risen in every London borough where the scheme is working, and in one [actually two, Chelsea and Deptford] the salvage returns have doubled.

Robert Edom was a Cog, with 'an enamel lapel badge in the shape of a cogwheel, in a group organised by an eccentric but very determined lady' who lived in his suburb of West Wickham in Kent.

'Sadly, as with most human institutions the Cogs were highly competitive. Sometimes Bill Oddy, always an entrepreneur, would take scrap even before the donor knew he had donated it. Bill took the view that if it wasn't nailed down with six-inch nails it was fair game. On one occasion I had to dissuade him from taking a metal air-raid shelter sign for scrap. His argument was that everyone knew where the air-raid shelter was anyway.

In my desperation to do my bit I even surrendered my shrapnel collection. I only retained the almost complete shiny metal nose cone from an anti-aircraft shell and I even felt guilty about that.

Then all of a sudden the eccentric lady disappeared. … [Her house] was locked up and deserted. … The depot was full of scrap that the Council had stopped collecting, and with no one to liaise with the Council or to organise us we lost our drive and direction. In no time at all the little Cogs stopped turning.'

A Ministry of Information leaflet issued in 1942 which 'specially concerns those between 14 and 18 years of age' reminded teenagers that 'no matter how young we are or how old we are there are jobs we can do for our country'. These included getting 'to know everything about the district where you live' so that in an emergency a child would know 'exactly where … the Air Raid Shelters, the First Aid Posts, the Fire Stations, the Telephone Boxes, the Police Stations, the Footpaths and the Short Cuts [are]. If you know where they are you may be able to save someone a few precious moments in an air raid.' But being useful 'begins at home' and children were encouraged to 'take charge of some of the air-raid precautions in your house – such as turning off the water and the gas when the sirens sound.' Some children took it upon themselves to monitor the family's fuel consumption since by 1941, despite an earlier glut, war industries were in desperate need of coal and householders were being urged to economise drastically. A north London schoolboy appointed himself:

fuel target overseer and checked the meter readings each week. I also made some cardboard rings to slip under the light switch cover in the shape of a face. The knob of the switch formed the nose, and I wrote 'please turn me off' round the edge.

School Cadets —
Practising "The Crawl"

Alex Macpherson

136

Apprentices to war. Alexander Macpherson's watercolour of 'School Cadets – practising "The Crawl"'.

Other children tried to help out by collecting sticks from woods and commons, and taking government advice literally by painting a 'plimsoll line' 'with a spot of enamel' round the inside of the bath so that no one was tempted to fill it higher that the recommended five inches.

Other useful tasks were recommended:

If you've got younger brothers or sisters, learn a few special games and tricks which will keep them from getting frightened during a raid. Learn to cook a simple meal under emergency conditions. … Help an elderly or invalid neighbour to put up an air-raid shelter. Learn all you can about first aid. … Join a group of young people in making splints and bandages or in knitting comforts for next winter. [Reginald Baker took up this suggestion: 'I learned to knit. We knitted scarves for soldiers in khaki wool. Just a straight scarf, nothing fancy.'] Be sure you know how to use the telephone efficiently. You never know when you'll want to send a vital message quickly.

Young people were also cautioned:

> Be Careful What You Say. Like everyone else, you will hear things that the enemy mustn't know. Keep that knowledge to yourself – and don't give away any clues. Keep Smiling. There's a lot of worry and grief in the world – and you can lessen it by being good-tempered and considerate. Keep Fit. … Save All You Can. Join a National Savings Group.

Many savings groups were organised by schools, and children effectively lent money to the government for the prosecution of the war.

Schools organised other wartime activities such as knitting parties, and collected books and magazines to send to the troops. After-school woodwork and sewing classes produced and mended toys and clothes for children who had lost their homes and possessions in air raids, and pupils also organised parties and picnics.

Boy Scouts and Girl Guides – and even occasionally Cubs and Brownies too – helped the war effort by collecting and sorting salvage, raising money for weapons, helping in military convalescent homes, making bandages out of old sheets, re-rolling bandages, acting as 'casualties' in Civil Defence exercises, learning to put out incendiary bombs and detect poison gas, and acting as messengers for the Home Guard ('not all fun when the invasion scare was on' as a history of the Girl Guide movement stresses).

A Girl Guide could earn a War Service Badge, and for every year of war service she could add another stripe to her award. Crosses in a calibrated range of metals – silver, bronze and gilt – were awarded for acts of bravery or fortitude. A Boy Scout could earn the Scout's National Service Badge provided he was over 14 and could demonstrate that he could write and deliver messages, had a specialised knowledge of the local area, could deal with an emergency and control panic, and had enrolled in some form of national service – which was required of all those aged between 16 and 18 by the end of 1941. More than 60,000 boys did so and there were some 180 jobs they could do including helping at ARP posts, serving as motor cycle messengers or telephone operators, escorting female ARP staff at night, directing traffic during the blackout, providing entertainments in shelters, assembling and distributing gas masks, filling and stacking sandbags, painting letters on tin helmets, acting as blood donors, working in first-aid posts, assisting with X-rays, erecting ambulance tents, filling in card indexes to log evacuees, cleaning houses requisitioned as billets, working as orderlies on barrage balloon sites, entertaining the troops, weeding and digging allotments, sharing their stalking and tracking skills with members of the Home Guard, running social events for refugees from overseas, shopping for the blind, painting kerb stones and railings white so they might be seen in the blackout, clearing snow from fire hydrants, mixing bleach paste, manufacturing home-made torch batteries, searching for domestic pets that had scarpered during a raid and binding up their wounds if necessary, knitting for the troops. … The list was inexhaustible.

Since the war had put paid to raising the school-leaving age, a boy could be a working man at 14. Here, an 18-year-old telephonist, E.D. Barry, with her 15-year-old brother, a messenger boy for Cable and Wireless, eat their lunch in a government-sponsored British restaurant.

137

Above: A typical scene in a south London ARP post. Boys and girls as young as 14 worked with the ARP manning the phones, taking messages between posts, logging incidents – all of which could be life-threatening work during the air raids.

Right: No. 230873 Second Subaltern Elizabeth Alexandra Mary Windsor. The heir to the throne, seen here with her sister, Princess Margaret Rose, registered with the ATS in February 1945. Although her rank was an honorary one, and she slept at home in Windsor Castle, rather than in barracks, her training in driving and vehicle maintenance was for real.

During raids Scouts and Guides often undertook hazardous tasks. They might be on duty to warn deaf people in the area of the air-raid warning siren or the All Clear. They might undertake fire-watching duties, alerting the emergency services when an incendiary bomb fell and helping put it out, and those who could ride a bike and knew the area well would act as messengers for the police and ARP wardens. Telephone lines would often be cut during heavy raids; the only way an ARP controller could communicate with the other posts in his area to direct the services to a particular incident was to send a messenger on a bicycle who would skid along the streets, a tin hat his or her only protection. At first messengers might be as young as 10, but when the raids came

it was raised to 16 for such responsible and dangerous work.

Harold Shipley's mother, who was a member of the St John's Ambulance Brigade near Hull, asked her 15-year-old son 'why don't you do something?' so he went along to the ARP warden's post and signed up as a messenger:

> I was one of the first local messengers. My first job was issuing gas masks [but when the Blitz came] my job was to run from warden's post to warden's post passing on messages. … Everyone complained that they'd heard the air-raid siren and they would go into the shelter, but then they never heard the All Clear. Maybe they

'Follow the yellow brick road … over the rainbow': **The Wizard of Oz**, *the 1939 musical starring Judy Garland, the cowardly lion, the scarecrow with no brain and the tin man with no heart, was the wartime child's must-see film – along with Walt Disney's* **Fantasia** *(1940) and his* **Dumbo** *(1941).*

Above: Sea Cadets. The signalling class practise semaphore at a training camp near Lake Windermere.

Right: The Boy Scouts' motto 'Be Prepared' seemed particularly apposite in wartime when 'wherever there is a job to be done, there you will find a Boy Scout'. In this case washing up after the evening meal at a fruit-picking camp in Kent.

140

were all asleep or something, but they all complained about it. So eventually they had us all going round ringing hand bells. They got hold of any school hand bell they could lay their hands on and we were all given an area and we had to get on our bikes and ride round in the blackout ringing these wretched bells. ... During the day I was a butcher's lad and I used to go round on my carrier bike and knock at people's doors and all I'd ever be asked was 'Where was the raid last night? Where were the bombs dropped?' And of course I didn't know.

Other young people put in war service with the Red Cross, the St John's Ambulance Brigade, the Boys' Brigade or the Church Lads' Brigade, while those who intended to join the army, navy, RAF or their female equivalents could enlist in cadet organisations to receive pre-service training. The Junior Training Corps (JTC) had been started when

Michael Ford's painting 'War Weapons Week in a Country Town' in which Brownies and Cubs can be seen taking part in a wartime fundraising event.

141

the War Office scrapped the Officers' Training Corps (OTC), which had been established in 1908 after the Boer War to produce potential army officers from the universities (senior division) and the public schools and independent grammar schools (junior division). On the outbreak of war the combined strength of the OTC was 30,000 cadets in 183 schools, but it was clear that the Corps would not produce the number of officers needed in wartime, and also that a more democratic system was needed. It was not only public schools that might be nurturing men of officer material. In future officers would also be commissioned from the ranks, not through direct entry from the OTC.

Schools that had not had an OTC (now JTC) could form a cadet unit under the auspices of the Army Cadet Force, and boys could officially sign up at 14, though many did so at 12. The Corps and the Force shared a training syllabus (that of the JTC) and boys were trained to peak physical fitness, drilled, taught map reading, fieldcraft, signalling and first aid.

Right: A Home Guard instructs a Boy Scout in rifle drill. On his arm, the Scout wears a War Scouts Service brassard.

There was an annual camp and the cadets learned to handle Lee Enfield rifles and later Sten guns and even Thompson sub-machine guns. Several JTS units signed up with the Home Guard in 1940 though that meant handing over their Lee Enfield rifles to the 'Dad's Army' who might still be training with pitchforks and broom handles. Some cadets, like those at Shrewsbury School, were integrated into Home Guard defence plans against invasion and patrolled railway lines with rifles and fixed bayonets.

The Sea Cadet Corps, which grew out of the pre-First World War Navy League, numbered some 9,000 cadets on the outbreak of war. Since the Royal and the Merchant Navies were in need of many more trained seamen, permission to expand was given and by September 1944 the number stood at 50,000. Sea Cadets were aged between 14 and 17 and were trained in the range of seaworthy skills and the leadership qualities needed by the naval services – though the Sea Cadets were often strapped for cash and the supply of boats to train in was sometimes rather limited. By 1943 it was clear that traditional seamanship needed to be underpinned with sophisticated technological training in such things as wireless telegraphy, naval aviation, and electrical and mechanical skills, and Sea Cadets made up the Royal Navy's shortfall of signallers and telegraphists.

The Air Training Corps was the pre-entry route to the RAF. It was formed in 1941 when it assumed control of training air cadets, who had previously been members of the Air Defence Cadet Corps (to which Brian Poole among others belonged until he was seduced by the activities of the Home Guard). From 18,489 members in 1941, the new Corps had increased to 200,000 by the end of 1942. The Battle of Britain undoubtedly made it the most glamorous of the services, and in August 1940 Captain W. E. Johns, the author of the Biggles stories and himself a bomber pilot at the end of the First World War, added to that lustre by writing regularly for the popular *Boy's Own Paper* about the daring exploits of the soon-to-be 'fly boys' of the ATC. The summit of most boys' ambition was to fly, and learning to handle gliders and visits to airfields and RAF stations were the acme of most Corps members' experience. At first an ATC recruit had to be 16, but by 1943 that had dropped to 15 years and 3 months, and by 1944 to 13 years 9 months. But entry was certainly no breeze: the service wanted technically able cadets and the syllabus was demanding. All recruits had to reach peak physical fitness and be competent at Morse code (up to four words a minute) and then could opt to learn aircrew skills, specialising in such things as navigation, anti-gas, aircraft identification, or technical subjects such as those a wireless operator, mechanic, flight mechanic or instrument repairer would need.

It was obvious that, although a government circular issued in 1941 recommended the registration of girls as well as boys over 16 for national services, there was a lamentable lack of training facilities for girls. In order to satisfy the desire of

'Somehow, in wartime, it just seemed right to be in uniform.' The Boys' Brigade stand to.

young women for pre-service training, the Girls' Training Corps (GTC), the Girls' Naval Training Corps (GNTC) and the Women's Junior Air Corps (WJAC) were formed in 1942, funded by local education authorities. The girls wore uniforms, but their talents and enthusiasms seemed on the whole to be channelled rather too readily into the tea-making and canteen-serving departments, though those in the WJAC did receive instruction in Morse code, first aid, anti-aircraft, radio location, signals, electrical and engineering operations – and inevitable office duties.

It had been intended to raise the school-leaving age to 15 but the war put paid to that, so many of those we would now think of as children were in full-time work. And in wartime that work could be dangerous and distressing. Ronald McGill recalls:

Above: Knit your own servicewoman. A pattern giving instructions for making a WAAF (Women's Auxiliary Air Force), an ATS (Auxiliary Territorial Service) or a WRNS (Women's Royal Naval Service) from 'oddments of 3 or 4-ply wool.'

> We had to leave school at 14. … Dad was anxious to get me into the Post Office [where he worked]. My schooling from 11 to 14 had been really very basic but the Post Office had agreed that the youngsters they took on would be sent to school for at least half a day a week. … Dad thought that was marvellous, my way to catch up. And it was … because most of my friends went straight into industry without any more schooling. … I was recruited as a telegram boy and I worked at Hammersmith, and the flying bombs were still coming so we had to ride around on our bikes delivering telegrams with our tin hats on. … There were 20 of us and we were responsible for delivering telegrams all over [Hammersmith]. And that's when

Reading the war

WILLIAM
AND AIR RAID
PRECAUTIONS

RICHMAL
CROMPTON

BANDIGES

AIR RADE
PRECORSHUN
JUNIER
BRANCH
ENTRUNCE
FREE

THE MOST POPULAR
William
BOY IN FICTION

144

' "Sleep?" echoed William in disgust. "I jolly well wouldn't waste an air raid sleepin' in it.'" ... He stopped and listened for a few moments. "That's a Dornier," he pronounced with an air of finality. "On the contrary, it's a cow," said Mr Brown, without looking up from his paper. ... "I bet that was a screaming bomb," said William. "It was the twelve-thirty letting off steam," said Mr Brown. ... "Gosh," said William excitedly, "I can hear bombs." But it was only the Bevertons arriving. Mrs Beverton ... and her daughter were both dressed in the latest siren suits, and had obviously taken great trouble with their make up and coiffures. ... [Mrs Beverton] had, moreover, used a new exotic perfume that made William cry out in genuine alarm

"Gas! Where's my gas mask?"'

Richmal Crompton's harum-scarum urchin, William Brown, was not the only popular children's book character to put his all into the war effort, getting involved with evacuees, salvage collection, ARP wardens, invasion threats, fire fighting and what he hoped was a German parachutist.

Bigglesworth, popularly known as Biggles, a slight, fair-haired, good-looking lad, still in his 'teens, but an acting Flight Commander, was soon in the front line too. Captain W.E. Johns, himself a former bomber pilot in the RAF in 1918, had first written about the insouciant Biggles in a story that appeared in his own magazine, Popular Flying, in 1932. Not long after war was declared, the daredevil flyer was in Norway – as was the action of war. The Battle of Britain found Biggles in command of a new squadron composed of 'star turns and officers who do not take kindly to discipline'. Next came Biggles Flies East and Biggles Defies the Swastika, written during the Blitz but suggesting the later reprisal 'saturation bombing' raids of 'Bomber' Harris. '"Well, I'm here and if I can put a spoke in the wheel of savages who drop bombs on helpless civilians, I certainly will," [Biggles] mused grimly.' And in 1940, in response to an Air Ministry request, Johns gave fictional birth to a WAAF, Joan Worralson, known as Worrals, who had some affinity with the aviatrix Amy Johnson, and like her 'yearned for adventure'.

Children's comics, as well as books, took

While Rupert's wondering what to play,
An airplane passes on its way.

145

more of a gung-ho than an escapist attitude to
wartime reading. Restrictions on paper meant
that many comics, including the pre-war
favourite *Tiger Tim's Weekly*, closed down, and
those that continued were much reduced in size
and their publication was sometimes
spasmodic. While *Chicks' Own* and other
comics for the tinies did not put on a tin hat,
Comic Cuts featured 'Big-Hearted Martha, our
ARP Nut'; 'Addie and Herman' (Adolf Hitler
and Hermann Goering) were *Dandy* stalwarts.
'Musso the Wop' (Mussolini) was a regular
in the Beano, as were Goering and Hitler
(under their own names). All usually
encoded a strong propaganda message for the
children of wartime Britain.

I really grew up, very quickly, because we were delivering all the death telegrams.

The girls in the delivery room used to say to us, 'This is a priority, and it's life or death, and it's a death.' And we were told that when we took the telegrams we were to take them and try and knock on [the house] on either side if you could. If you turned into a road you saw the curtains twitch, we were feared, there's no other word for it. And we were only 14. And we knew what we were carrying. …

I knocked on one door and there was no reply … in a small road near Hammersmith Bridge. And the lady looked out, she must have seen that I was knocking on either side, and she came out and said 'That's for me isn't it?' I said 'Yes, number …' whatever it was, I can't remember. And she fainted, just fell down on the ground. And the two little kiddies ran out, and I was 14, you know, how do I deal with that? She hadn't even opened the envelope. And I managed to get another neighbour to run along and they managed to pull the lady into her house. And they opened [the telegram] and it

Above: A Somerset farmyard scene showing a haystack and chickens being fed, painted by D. Coxwell, an evacuee from Farrance Street School, Limehouse, in the East End of London.

146

Right: War Savings propaganda. A drawing by 10-year-old Ron Cox for the purpose of war savings – though interestingly these are being tossed into to 'Uncle Sam's' Stars and Stripes top hat.

was her husband, and he had been killed.

And I just stood there. I didn't know what to do. It was such a terrible thing, I just grew up very quick. And we were getting this four of five times a day. … Sometimes I'd cycle round the block four or five times before I knocked on the door. It's a silly thing to do, but I thought it gave them a bit longer before they knew. But they always knew. As soon as they saw the uniform they knew.

At 18 years of age a young man was liable for military service unless he was in a reserved occupation; from December 1941 a young, single woman (aged 20, later lowered to 19) would be liable for conscription too, or direction into war work, unless she likewise was already doing an essential job. But even before that time came, many young people had already served a tough apprenticeship in the realities of war.

Children at an Oxfordshire village school buying savings stamps from their teacher to help the war effort.

6

'For the duration'

'D'you know,' said William [Brown of Richmal Crompton's *Just William* books] thoughtfully at breakfast. 'I don't seem to remember the time there wasn't a war,'

'Don't be ridiculous, William,' said his mother. 'It's hardly lasted two years and you're 11 years old, so you must remember the time when there wasn't a war. All the same,' she added with a sigh, 'I know what you mean.'

The Blitz effectively ended – for the time being – after the heaviest raid of the war on London on 10 May 1941, when well over 1,000 people were killed in a single night in London and more than 2,000 injured. But that did not mean that there were no more attacks on the home front: 'tip-an'-run' raids harried ports and industrial centres throughout 1942 and 1943, and from April 1942 came the so-called 'Baedeker raids' in retaliation for British bombing of the German cities of Lübeck and Rostock. Fierce air attacks were mounted on Bath, Canterbury, Exeter, Norwich and York, places supposedly awarded stars in the pre-war German Baedeker guidebook as being of outstanding historic interest.

On 20 January 1943, ten-year-old Joan Burridge was walking home when she was fired on by a German plane. 'A passing postman threw me against a garden wall while he crouched down by his bicycle.' The plane seemed to be aiming directly at Sandhurst Road School in Catford, south-east London. Most of the children were in the dining hall in the centre of the school when the bomb dropped. Within minutes the school was a mass of fire; children, many of them hurt, were screaming and running in and out of the gardens of nearby houses.

A woman who had watched the plane go over and hurried to the scene on her bike 'dismounted because of the rubble which was strewn across the road. Then to my horror, I saw several children's bodies and limbs of the ones that had been playing in the playground.'

Children's bodies and those of some of their teachers lie covered by tarpaulins after the bombing of Sandhurst Road School, Catford, on 20 January 1943. The censor refused to pass this photograph for publication, regarding it as too upsetting for public morale.

Inconsolable parents and friends of the victims of the Sandhurst Road School bombing at the communal funeral at Hither Green cemetery. Over 7,000 mourners attended.

149

Outside the school, shocked parents and relatives stood in stunned silence as rescue workers, police and volunteers clawed desperately at the debris, trying to release any child that might be trapped beneath the bricks and girders. A policeman who had volunteered to help, Sergeant Norman Greenstreet, found the body of his own eight-year-old son in the rubble. Gunner Charles Allford, who had fought in the First World War and volunteered for the Second, was on leave at the family home just round the corner from the school, which his two young daughters attended. He rushed to the school and among the debris found the body of Brenda, aged five. 'Her forehead and her cheek were badly cut. Her little arm lay over her face as if to protect herself. I am glad it was me who found her,' he told a *Daily Telegraph* reporter. Gunner Allford was finally persuaded to go home and several hours later the body of his other daughter, Lorina, aged seven, was discovered. Two bothers, Dennis Barnard aged ten and Ronald aged nine, were killed; so were Anne and Judith Biddle, both aged five, and Eunice and Pauline Davies, aged nine and seven. A total of 38 children aged between five and 15 died in the terrible incident, along with six members of staff. Although a boys' school in Petworth in Surrey had been hit in a similar tip-an'-run raid four months previously with the loss of 31 lives, Catford was the first daylight raid on London since 1940. It resulted in massive publicity and outrage, with local residents claiming that the school had been deliberately targeted. The funerals of most of the children were held the following Saturday; 'the flower-laden hearses seemed to stretch for miles' and many were buried in a communal grave. The service, which was

A Morrison shelter (named after the Home Secretary, Herbert Morrison) which began to be distributed in March 1941, towards the end of the Blitz. The heavy reinforced steel shelter proved invaluable to flat-dwellers and anyone without a garden. It was intended to be used as a table during the day and as a cage shelter when the air raids came.

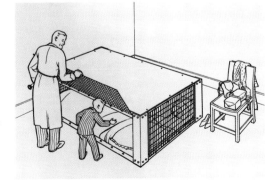

150

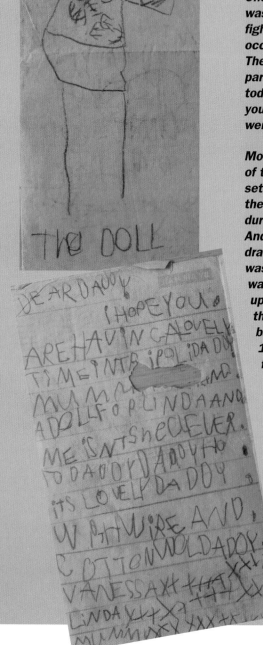

'Missing you all ...'

One of the irrecoverable losses of the war was the fact that fathers who were away fighting had to rely on letters and the occasional photograph of their children. They missed the pleasures and trials of parenting, in many cases for years, as toddlers grew into schoolchildren, and young teenagers into adults while they were away.

Mothers were usually assiduous in writing of the children's small advances and setbacks: the first tooth, the first words, the good school report, the arm broken during cricket practice, the career plans. And most would include letters and drawings from the children. Peggie Phillips was no exception. Her husband, John, who was 29 when war broke out, was called up in the late summer of 1940, when their daughter Vanessa was two, and baby Linda just a few months old. In 1942 he was posted to North Africa and fought in the Battle of El Alamein.

The couple wrote regularly. Peggie sent news of the children's doings: Vanessa's artistic prowess, Linda beginning to crawl, how she was trying to find somewhere suitable for them all to live after the war. She told him about the bomb that fell on the depository where all the Phillips' furniture and effects – except their precious piano – were stored, their friends, her hopes of picking up again the dancing career she had had before the

children were born, how much she was missing him. John's letters were full of the frustrations and amusements of army life. Of how it all seemed such a waste of time, but how he was managing to keep busy, using his talents to paint camouflage and sketch his fellow soldiers, how concerned he was about his family during the air raids, and how hard it was to be apart.

John Phillips wrote often to his small daughters too. He was a graphic artist in civilian life and his letters were enlivened with sketches of his life as a soldier in far-flung places, and what he imagined his family might be doing while he was away.

The story should have had a happy ending: the family reunited. But it did not. Gunner Phillips was killed fighting in Italy on 26 November 1943. And as his wife was promising her small daughters that she hoped this would be the 'last Christmas they would have to spend without Daddy', the last letter that she had written to her husband was already being returned stamped 'It is regretted that ...'

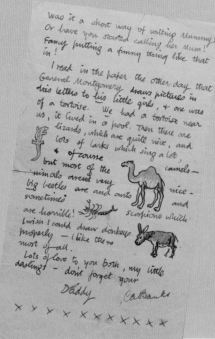

Above: Not only were busy wartime mothers expected to make their children's clothes out of their own whenever possible, and mend them when they wore out. They were also advised to reinforce the garments even before the children had worn them to give them 'twice the life.'

Right: 'WVS Clothing Exchange, 1943', by Evelyn Gibbs.

conducted by the Bishop of Southwark, was attended 'by local dignitaries and most of the local population', some 7,000 in all.

Not very far from the scene of the Catford tragedy, more than 60 children under the age of 16 were killed on 3 March 1943. But this time it was not enemy action that was directly to blame. An attack was expected in retaliation for a major RAF bombing raid on Berlin on 1 March. On the evening of 3 March the Alert sounded at 8.17 p.m. At that time there were already some 500 people sheltering on the platform of Bethnal Green tube station in east London, 78 feet below ground. Reginald Baker who, with his family, was a habitué knew it well:

> The tube from Liverpool Street wasn't built any further than Mile End then. The rail lines weren't actually there. There were just concrete slabs, so they built bunk beds. At night I used to put my shoes in the slots where the cables are now. There were bunk beds on either side, three high, in alphabetical order. We were C 71, 72 and 73. So I slept in the top, me dad in the middle, me mother in the bottom. And I remember the smell of the chemical toilets down there to this day. And the warm air rushing along the tunnels.

Fully anticipating a major raid that night, far more people than had normally been taking to the tubes in recent months converged on the small booking hall at Bethnal Green station, waiting to descend the single, narrow, dimly lit staircase to the platform. Suddenly new rocket batteries opened up in nearby Victoria Park, emitting a noise louder and stranger than anyone had heard before. Panic ensued as East Enders tried to pile into the station, thinking an attack was imminent. Near the bottom of the steps, a young woman clutching her baby lost her footing and fell. Others fell on her and those pressing to get down the stairs, unable to see what had happened, probably presumed

The WVS Clothing Exchange proved a godsend for mothers with growing children when clothes and shoes were put 'on the ration' in June 1941 and it was a struggle to keep your offspring warm and decent.

153

that the gates had been shut and pushed and heaved forwards. Within 90 seconds 173 people, 62 of them children, had been crushed and suffocated to death.

Reginald Baker was in the crowd trying to get down the stairs that night:

> It was terrible. My sister and I were very fortunate to be pulled out from that pile of bodies still alive, because if we'd been there much longer, we'd have all been dead. … What the wardens saw was unbelievable. In those days most men wore hob-nailed boots and so they found the imprint of hob-nailed boots on children's faces. Unbelievable. There was a whole family wiped out. They were called Mead, mum, dad, two sisters and the son who was in my class at school at the time, they were all killed.

An official enquiry – the results of which were not published until January 1945 for fear of inciting the enemy to mount further panic-inducing attacks and of damaging civilian morale in London – concluded that no one person was to blame for the panic of a crowd of some 1,500 people. It was a tragic accident, though it was one waiting to happen, given the lack of police or trained Civil Defence wardens (as ARP wardens had been retitled in recognition of how wide their responsibilities now were) present, the narrowness of the stairway, the bad lighting and absence of crush barriers or even a hand rail. 'London Transport wouldn't allow £86 12s to have a wall built round the entrance which might have stopped it; they just said "we'll use old doors from bombed-out houses,"' claims Reg Baker bitterly. No major bomb incidents were reported in the East End that night.

Concern about such incidents and anxiety about when the night-time raids might start again in earnest were compounded by wider problems. Allied forces had suffered almost nothing but defeats, setbacks and losses at sea, in Europe, in North Africa and the Far East until the Battle of El Alamein in November 1942. Even that, Churchill cautioned, was certainly not the 'beginning of the end'; all that could be hoped was that it might be 'the end of the beginning'. And in its less dramatic forms the dismal war of attrition seeped into people's lives. Ingenuity was needed to feed a family on inadequate rations while the demands of war production pushed people to work even harder and longer, and forced many women to juggle two, if not three, jobs. The pervasive dreariness of the continuous blackout limited every activity. There were endless transport difficulties, with petrol all but unavailable to the private motorist, depleted public services and crowded trains and buses. These privations, and the increasing shortages of everything from babies' feeding bottles to saucepans, new books to children's toys, could grind down an already tired and often dispirited population. Those middle years were, as the more poetic were inclined to sigh, 'a lightless tunnel'.

Another belt tightening – almost literally this time – had come on Whit Sunday 1 June 1941, when it was announced on the wireless that clothes rationing would take effect that day. Since there were no clothes coupons, shops would accept margarine coupons in their stead for the time being. Subsequently, everyone was issued with a special clothing coupon book in addition to the food ration book. Every possible article of clothing

Patricia Violet Wright, whose mother was killed in an air raid, sucks her pencil and tries to think what to write in her thank-you letter for her new shoes sent over from the United States.

A 'make do and mend' rabbit fashioned from odd scraps of used fabric.

155

Above: Nothing wasted. A child's sun dress made from the silk on which maps given to RAF pilots were printed. After the war these were sold off to the public for 5/11d.

Above right: Encouraged by the sewing instructress, three-year-old Dorothy Bates models an outfit made by her mother to a 'Make Do and Mend' class.

156

required coupons except hats and industrial overalls (though these came under the scheme later). Since children wore their clothes out faster, and also outgrew them, children's clothes required fewer coupons so their allocation would go further (and anyway they used less material and thus involved fewer factories in producing clothes and shoes rather than war matériel). At first everyone received 66 coupons a year, which it was reckoned would allow people to buy around two-thirds as much clothing as before the war. In 1942 the ration was reduced to 60 coupons and to 48 in 1943, and was cut down even more at the end of the war.

Baby clothes were initially coupon-free but within two months they too were incorporated into the rationing scheme. Pregnant women, who were not given any extra allowance for maternity clothes, were issued with 50 (later increased to 60) coupons to buy a layette for their baby – or the materials to make it, since knitting matinée jackets and bootees and smocking baby gowns was a frequent 'expectant' pastime, particularly for middle-class women. As soon as the baby was born, she or he was entitled to the full 60 coupons, though many mothers complained that this was nowhere near enough, particularly as a packet of terry towelling nappies took 24 coupons. The Board of Trade, which administered the system, was deeply unsympathetic; one (male?) civil servant commented that the 'shortage of napkins may sorely afflict the infant, but it looks as though this has always been one of the penalties of infancy.'

Dissatisfaction with the coupon allowance for children rumbled on, and in 1942 all children were granted a supplementary 10 coupons per year, with an extra 20 coupons for adolescents and 'outsize' children: those under 13 who were exceptionally tall or heavy for their age. More than 2 million children born after 1929 were weighed and measured at school to see if they qualified for this extra allowance.

Few mothers were satisfied with these rather measly concessions, however, and throughout the war the Ministry of Information's Home Intelligence reports monitoring morale and highlighting issues that were preoccupying the public showed that children's clothing continued to be a major issue – particularly when the overall coupon allowance was cut back to 48. Shoes were the biggest worry, and this was said in some areas to be 'affecting school attendance'. In the summer of 1943 the situation was reported to be 'acute and becoming a real anxiety to mothers'. The Board of Trade again pronounced: this time maintaining that the coupons would enable the purchase of three pairs of shoes a year. This met with incredulity from parents of growing children; the Good Housekeeping Institute recommended that a child needed three pairs of shoes at a time, rather than for a whole year. It emphasised what mothers already knew, that it was 'most important … that a child should never wear badly-fitting footwear: shoes that are either too small or too big definitely harm the feet and should not be allowed.'

A Home Intelligence report on comments across the country in the summer of 1943 concluded that the Board was showing:

no sign whatever of understanding the difficulties of the growing child. … 'It would be interesting to know whether there are any real family men in the administration of this sphere.' Mothers who have already been sacrificing their own

coupons for their children's clothing 'have no idea how they will manage in the future'. ... Footwear difficulties [were] a 'major problem'. ... 'Shoes are responsible for more parental worries and grey hairs than all the air raids'. ... Children are being kept from school ... [and] in Newcastle 'they are to be seen running barefoot in the streets, after a lapse of 20 years'.

There were of course a great number of cast-offs – shoes included – that were routinely handed around among family and friends. In October 1942 an enterprising schoolmaster at Ewell in Surrey, noticing what problems his pupils' mothers were having

Right: A child's playpen on display at an exhibition of utility furniture. Despite the no-frills edict for such furniture, wooden counting beads were still permitted on this item.

in keeping them decently clothed and shod, asked the WVS to help him run a clothing exchange. It was obviously such a sensible idea that the Board of Trade took notice and recruited the WVS, who were already running clothing stores and distributing gifts of clothing from home and overseas to those who had been left bereft by air raids, to set up similar exchanges all over the country. There were soon nearly 400 of them, and mothers could turn in clothes that were 'outgrown but not outworn' in exchange for others of the right size. Clothes had to be clean, and no money changed hands, but there were always more piles of baby clothes on offer than trousers and overcoats for adolescent boys.

Given wartime shortages, many of the clothes brought in to be swapped might be clean but were often pretty worn, so soon 'Make Do and Mend' sessions were held in most WVS clothing exchanges so that mothers could be taught how to repair and cannibalise their children's garments. This was in line with a government campaign and the saws of its irritatingly perky cartoon character, 'Mrs Sew and Sew', who tried to make all this darning and patching and turning sides to middle sound fun rather than the tiresome wartime necessity that it was. The Board of Trade produced a booklet, and numerous announcements appeared in the press and women's magazines about Making Do and Mending: worn jumpers should be unravelled and reknitted into something else; hopelessly felted or matted wool could be 'cut like cloth' and made into 'children's coats, capes, hoods or mittens'; outgrown shoes could be turned into 'sandals' by having the toes cut out; the tops of a worn-out pair of wool stockings 'will make cosy underpants for a small boy'. Worn men's clothes could be turned into women's – 'plus fours will make an excellent skirt' – while both could be down-scaled for children. 'Either daddy's pyjama jacket or his trousers will yield enough material for a pair of pyjamas for a two-year-old [since] … for some reason or another a man will often only wear out the coat or the trousers.' Even pyjama legs could make a child's vest; worn bath towels could be cut up for babies'

Housewife

NOVEMBER

9d

1944

nappies, and it only took a little ingenuity to turn a battered felt hat into a pair of child's slippers. Some little girls went out to tea wearing dresses made from architect's plans that had been soaked long enough for the paper to dissolve, and a few little boys might be seen playing conkers dressed in shiny, serge, pin-striped shorts.

It wasn't just children's clothes that were in short supply. In August 1944 there was an acute shortage of babies' bottles just at the moment when the birth rate, which had been depressed in the early years of the war, was beginning to rise again in anticipation of peace. New mothers were reported to be 'bitter' because 'in some cases they have had to buy bottles they do not need in order to get a single teat' (strangely it seemed that there was ample rubber available for contraceptives).

There was also an acute shortage of cots, high chairs and playpens. All of these were made of wood, and wood was in particularly short supply since it was needed for such

War effort. One solution to the problem of childcare for mothers employed on war production was for a friend or neighbour to care for their children while they were at work. Here Mrs Dart looks after six children of working mothers in her own home in Bristol.

Looking after the children

In the autumn of 1941, the Minister of Labour, Ernest Bevin, wrote, 'I have to look to married women not previously employed to supply much of the necessary additional power from industry. From that point of view the provision of the care of children is now a matter of the first importance to the war effort.'

Before the war, nurseries had been regarded primarily as a safety net for inadequate parenting, rather than as an early educational and socialising opportunity for young children. Now all that was about to change. Manpower surveys had shown that as many woman as possible – including those with children under 14 living at home – were needed in the factories or in other jobs to release younger 'mobile' women to go into the forces or to be directed into munitions. Yet it was still generally accepted that a woman's place – and certainly a mother's – was in the home, caring for her family. A campaign was mounted to encourage neighbours and grandmothers to look after other women's children, but that was not going to be a sufficient solution.

In July 1940 the redoubtable Lady Reading, founder of the WVS and Chairman of the National Society of Day Nurseries, summed up the situation in an article in Picture Post.

If anything good has come out of this war, it is the fact that at last the need and the value of day nurseries has been forced on us. ... Married women, as well as unmarried ones, are taking their share in Britain's war effort. And a woman cannot be expected to pull her weight in a factory if she is worrying about her children all day. ... The solution to the problem is day nurseries. ... Mothers bring their children on their way to

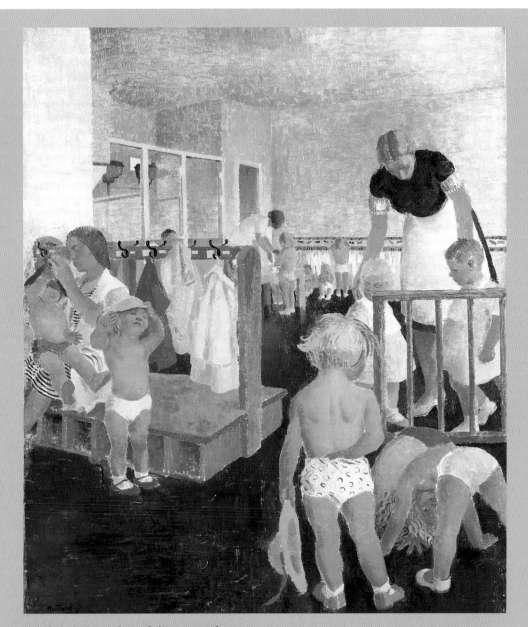

Above: 'A Nursery School for War Workers' Children' by Elsie Dalton Hewland.

work in the morning, call for them on their way home at night. Meanwhile under the care of a fully qualified matron and staff, they are washed, put to sleep and guarded all day.

Their mothers pay according to their needs, usually 1/6d a day, which includes three meals, and when they call for their children, they can get lots of advice from matron for the same, inclusive cost.

Lady Reading went on to to suggest how a group of mothers could set up their own nursery school:

in a light, airy building, [using] simple home-made furniture. ... Fruit crates can be turned into cradles and cupboards. A pot of paint decks your furniture in gay colours. A few simple toys, coloured beads, balls and plasticine complete your outfit. ... [But] the State must pay for the initial capital expenditure and should give a maintenance grant as well. Money has to be found for essential war services – the care of our future citizens under war conditions is surely an essential service.

To maximise wartime production, factories had to work round the clock and from mid-1942 some day nurseries in industrial areas were permitted to operate for 24 hours a day, while other children were boarded in residential nurseries – though mothers complained that these were 'really only for waifs and strays, or at any rate not for the children of women who earn a fair wage by working 11 hours a day in the factory.'

Despite the fact that government-sponsored nurseries increased from just 14 in October 1940 to 1,245 by July 1943, they were regarded by many in official circles as little more than 'cloakrooms' where children could be deposited while mothers worked. So it was hardly surprising that so many were summarily closed down at the end of the war when women's labour was no longer needed to the same extent.

Below: Nurseries in Tottenham, north London, and Birmingham for the children of mothers working in wartime.

wartime imperatives as building ships and planes, shelters and bridges – and much of it was imported anyway. Again much baby equipment was handed down and might conceivably be bought second hand (no coupons were required for second-hand goods, though there was a government-imposed limit on the price charged).

It was hardly practical to ration furniture – say one bed, two chairs and a table every other year – since most people would only need to buy the occasional item, while 'bombees' might have to replace every stick of furniture they had owned. In February 1941 a 'utility' scheme was introduced for both furniture and clothes, which were to be produced to a specified, no-frills design. The aim was to provide the public with a serviceable and good-value (though limited) range of goods that required the minimum of both materials and labour in their manufacture. Both the furniture and the clothes would be stamped with the 'utility mark' of two C-shaped wedges and the number 41, and no one could buy furniture without producing a 'Certificate of Need'. 'Need' included being made homeless and possession-less as a result of enemy action, getting married and setting up home for the first time, or, in practice, having a baby, since no permit was required for nursery furniture, though it was by no means always easy to obtain.

Verily Anderson had two very small daughters and she and her husband were renting:

[a] pleasant family house in St John's Wood, north London. … Only one other house in the road was inhabited. Behind us a long crescent of over a hundred huge empty houses was slowly disintegrating, with the aid of the weather and former bombing. It was an eerie street to go along, with some of its ornate houses lying flat in their own gardens. … The furniture we took out of store was only enough for a small flat, and now we had a four-storeyed ten-roomed house to fill. But in the deserted gardens of the crescent I had seen broken chairs and tables and bedsteads. If the shops were empty, I knew where to go to get what we needed. … Into our garden had been blown a broken lawn-sprinkler, which we converted into a standard lamp for our drawing room …

[but] a nursery fire-guard was something impossible to find in any shop. The day I stepped out of a bombed site with one in my arms, I walked straight into a policeman. I thought instantly of the notices saying that looters might be shot. The policeman shook his head in a disappointed way as though he expected better of me.

'I know,' I said. 'I'm ready. You can shoot me.'

'It's not that, miss,' he said. 'I've had my eye on it to take home after dark for my own toddler.'

'Take it,' I said, holding it out to him.

'No, miss,' he said sadly. 'You got it first.' And he continued on his beat.

LEND TO DEFEND HIS RIGHT TO BE FREE BUY DEFENCE BONDS

for obtain...

Toys from the rag bag

Sally

Robert Rabbit

Ernie Elephant

Sambo

54

55

Housewife *December 1942*

163

Children missed out on many things during the Second World War: security, schooling, holidays, treats – and toys. With factories increasingly turned over to war production, and government restrictions on what could be produced and what raw materials could be used, toys – particularly those made using wood, rubber, plastics or synthetics – were increasingly hard to buy. By 1941 the supply of toys had fallen some 75 per cent compared with pre-war levels – and it could be heartrending for parents to be unable to find the toys they would have liked to give their children at Christmas and birthdays. Mass-Observation reported in 1942 that of the parents they quizzed just under three-quarters either planned or were forced to economise on cards, food and presents, but that the other quarter were determined not to have an economy Christmas but to make it as 'normal as possible'. As the war dragged on, children were having to be grateful for an orange as a present, plus a hand-me-down toy that had been mended or repainted or, if they had dextrous parents, perhaps a new doll or soft toy fashioned out of scraps of material or wool, or a toy farm, fort or cart banged together using oddments of wood and painted with whatever – often unsuitable – colour of paint could be found lurking in pre-war tins.

It was not just the amount of toys that had changed. It was the sort of toys too. As with the games children played, so too with their toys, the effect of war was pervasive. As early in the war as Christmas 1939, the toy buyer at Harrods store in Knightsbridge had noticed:

164

A child's drawing of tanks in battle by Henry Ellison.

Henry Ellison.

a spate of toys [and] games associated in one way or another with the war. ... Outstanding among the toys which are clearly an outcome of the war are the model trench scenes and troops in action and models of the Maginot Line [the supposedly impenetrable French border fortifications] ... peopled with figures of both the French and British armies [and showing] barbed-wire entanglements and bursting shells culminating in the visible fortification of the line itself, four gun turrets with cotton wool to indicate gunfire. ... Among the games, playing cards have been adapted to imaginary troops or ships or units of the air force. ... Lead soldiers, even of the enemy, have gone well, although they in particular are, of course, old-fashioned. Uniformed dolls and model ARP units [are] popular too and overheard conversations indicate the desire of adults to move with the times when gift buying. A woman member of the AFS [Auxiliary Fire Service] for example was overheard trying to buy a boy of six a model fire engine.

Two years later, Selfridges toy department reported that there 'was nothing new on the market, nothing at all. All the tricycles had been sold and there were no teddy bears at all – and everyone seems to want a teddy bear and they just don't

Prisoners of war

When the news of Italy's surrender was announced on 8 September 1943, there were some 75,000 Italian prisoners of war (POWs) in Britain. Soon the uniform they all wore would sport a distinctive orange 'bulls eye' on the back for instant recognition if they tried to escape. At first the POWs lived in camps, but gradually regulations were relaxed and the Italians, the majority of whom worked on farms, were allowed to live in the community and have some contact with the British people.

It was often children who got on best with the POWs. Teenage girls were taken with the good looks of many and their way of calling out 'Ah, carissima — we love you', while younger children were the beneficiaries of the characteristic Italian fondness for bambini, and their generosity to their captors' children when so many were desolate at being parted from their own families back home in Italy.

165

Above: Italian POWs working on a West Country farm make friends with evacuee children from London.

Right: Toy rocking horse made by an Italian POW for a British child.

The child within us all. American GIs carry dolls, probably won at a shooting range, through London streets.

seem to be making them.' Harrods had 'a few teddy bears at 10/- though they are selling fast – they'll all be gone soon,' while the children's tea sets 'looked as if they were 1901 stock'.

At Hamleys the manager reported that:

> trenches are sold in sections and can be pinned together. People don't buy forts now. They buy these. … Mr Reynolds [the manager] unpacked a toy howitzer which he explained was an improvement on last year's model. It fired lead shells at three ranges, 6, 10 and 12 feet. It was breech loaded and had a mechanism for elevation, together with a range finder.

Hamleys were also selling 'a coastal defence gun which fired wooden shells'; a scale model of a Hawker Hurricane, 'one of the RAF's latest interceptor fighters. Camouflage finish and correct markings'; or a Supermarine Spitfire 'reported to be the world's fastest interceptor fighter. Fitted with retractable undercarriage and camouflaged (both 4/- in kit form or 8/9d for the made-up model).' Present buyers could bag an anti-aircraft gun: 'a really fine model firing a wooden shell and … manipulated similar to a full-sized gun. Loading and firing is semi-automatic (8/6d)'; or a barrage balloon unit: 'this represents the latest type of captive balloon [which] can be raised or lowered by means of the winch on the lorry (10/11d)'.

At Marks and Spencer in North End Road, Fulham, a brisk trade was being done in camouflage helmets which, the manager explained, were selling to children with fathers or brothers who had been called up. At Harrods the story was much the same. The 'first thing to go, and in large numbers, has been khaki suits and uniforms both for officers and forage', and the toy buyer had no idea when he'd be able to get any more. 'Indeed the question of obtaining raw materials to make toys was a very serious one.' Whereas there hadn't been much of an increase in the sale of lead soldiers themselves, 'all the appurtenances and accessories such as sectional trenches, pill boxes, sand bagging, camouflage netting and entanglements' were going like hot cakes.

There seemed no escape: the jigsaws that were flying off the shelves depicted 'Epics of War' and reproduced sketches by famous war artists 'and are officially approved by the Ministry of Information'. The first four titles were *The First Air Attack on a British Convoy Ends in German Disaster*; *The RAF Reconnaissance Planes Beat Off German Fighters*; *Navy Drives Off German Bombers*; and *BEF* [British Expeditionary Force] *Moves Up to the Front*. '14" x 10", over 200 interlocking pieces. Price 6d.' There might perhaps be some respite from war with 'old-fashioned games' such as chess, draughts, Halma and Ludo, which were reported to be selling well, as were 'gambling games such as Beetle, Snap, Old Maid etc.' though even here new games such as Submarine Hunt and Tri-tactics, Battle of the River Plate, ARP ('a topical game playing on the same principle as snakes and ladders – denotes wardens and others duties in the event of an air raid (2/11d)') and Aeroplane Shooting ('the shooting game of the year five aeroplanes flying in formation and attached to a scenic background are shot down by means of a gun firing elastic bands. Safe and harmless (2/11d)') were drawing great interest, as was 'L'Attaque – a war game from the last war'.

When it came to girls there was 'a good supply of expensive dolls but rag or stuff dolls were more difficult to find – though there was a considerable line in Negro babies and Hamleys had many dolls in period costume'. But maybe the wartime child really did want to cuddle an ATS, WRNS or WAAF or a Land Army doll ('smart corduroys in fawn, green pullover and hat and white shirt') or an AFS doll ('called from the Fire Station in full service kit') or even 'a dog in uniform' – a snip at 15/-.

There were, however, virtually 'no presents for babies (rubber, celluloid or stuff balls, dolls, ducks etc.) and no clockwork toys. … Children under four will be the chief sufferers in wartime,' predicted the Hamleys buyer sadly.

However, in the dark days of those mid-wartime years, there was a glimmer of hope, both for the nation and for the nation's children. On 7 December 1941 the Japanese bombed the US Pacific Fleet at anchor in Pearl Harbor in Hawaii. Winston Churchill was profoundly relieved to know that as result of this 'the United States was in the war, up to the neck and in to the death … after 17 months of lonely fighting … We had won the war. England would live; Britain would live. … Once again in our long island history we should emerge, however mauled or mutilated, safe and victorious.' The next day, President Roosevelt, who had been doggedly trying to edge a reluctant United States into joining the Allied fight against Hitler, declared war on Japan. On 11 December Germany and Italy declared war on the United States, and Churchill was able to extract a commitment from Roosevelt to a 'Europe First' strategy and a promise that US troops would be sent to Britain forthwith.

The GIs were a revelation. As a Home Office report put it in 1945:

> To girls brought up on the cinema, who copied the dress, hair styles and manners of Hollywood stars, the sudden influx of Americans speaking like the films, who actually lived in the magic country, and who had plenty of money, at once went to the girls' heads. The Americans' … proneness to spoil a girl, to build up, exaggerate, talk big, and act with generosity and flamboyance, helped to make them the most attractive of boyfriends.

A Plymouth woman who was 17 when the GIs arrived at a barracks near Devonport in 1943 recalled:

> My first two boyfriends were American and I 'dated' some others. Some of us in our mid-teens had never really never known any English boys except of our own age and these soldiers seemed so glamorous to us all. … They were easy

New World ways. GI Sergeant Bert Spence, stationed in Britain for the build-up to D-Day, teaches a British schoolboy to play 'the all-American game of baseball.'

167

to talk to, speaking very naturally and casually, unlike the reticent, sometimes sniggery youths we knew.

The Yanks bought a cornucopia to young English girls starved of luxuries. 'They were equipped up the eyebrows with scented soap, cigarettes, food, sweets and dozens of things we had not seen for years. It was like Christmas.' Most GIs were young, far from home for the first time, and with money jingling in their pockets (an American private was paid £3 8s 9d a week while he was in the UK, as compared with the 14/- weekly pay of a British soldier of equivalent rank) they could be very generous to their British girlfriends, sourcing confectionery, cosmetics and nylons from the lavishly stocked PXs (Post Exchanges, the US version of the NAAFI).

They also brought fun. Averil Martin was only 18 when the Americans arrived in Sussex. Although she was too young to go to the GI dances, she borrowed some make-up and, in the absence of nylons, painted her legs an ochre colour with pancake make-up, pretended that she was 18 and went along to dance with the 'dudes':

Everything in England seemed so dull and corny in comparison. Their music was fantastic. I loved jitterbugging. I won a contest. We used to make these dresses with short, pleated skirts and when we danced they'd flare up round our waists ...who wants to listen to some schmaltzy sentimental music when they're young and can dance to 'Take the A-Train' with the Yanks?

The quaint customs of a small island. American GIs on a visit to Christ's Hospital School (known as the Blue Coat School) near Horsham in Sussex watch the public school boys march into the dining hall – a daily one o'clock ritual.

Connie Stanton, who lived near Bedford where there were several US Army Air Force bases, was even younger:

> I didn't want the GIs to know that I was only twelve and a half. I wanted them to think that I was 16. My school was so near the base that the Snowdrops [US military police, so-called because of their white helmets] could see us in the playground … so I used to keep right out of sight so they wouldn't recognise me … and then I'd watch for the 'liberty bus' [or 'passion wagon' as it was also known] outside the American Red Cross in Bedford come to collect the local girls and take them to the base for a dance. … I'd heard that Glenn Miller was coming … and I didn't know who he was then, but I was *determined* to hear him play. So I stood outside the gate all dressed up and waited while the boyfriend of an older girl took her in and then came back to escort me in. Of, course, my mother never knew. … Whenever I hear 'Moonlight Serenade' now, I still remember that evening. … It was *wonderful*.

Norma Fisher, who was 'plump, and wore the front of her hair in a roll called a bang', lived in the same tenement as Barbara Roose, who recalls:

> [She] was an expert at the jitterbug. Her performance with her Yank boyfriend could clear the floor and raise applause at the Lyceum ballroom in the Strand. …

Anglo-American relations. Some 200 British children, each in some way a victim of the war, are entertained by US troops on Thanksgiving Day, 27 November, 1942.

Understanding your allies. Above: A school prefect reads a passage of C.F. Strong's **The Story of America** *to his classmates (above). Before the war American history was hardly taught in British schools, and many young people's only concept of America was from the cinema. Right: A game of flag identification.*

170

I begged Norma to teach me how to jitterbug. She finally gave in … and we spent a few Saturday afternoons practising like pet elephants in the wash house on the landing. … If the doors were kept tightly shut, even the tones of [Norma's friend] Betty singing 'In the Mood' became muffled. What joy!

With the advent of the Americans Norma and Betty had managed to acquire some … nylons. They came to see us full of excitement. They were indeed beautiful, unbelievably sheer and shiny and at the same time so strong. Mum tactfully added a word of advice to Norma not to get too involved with the Yanks. Norma, full of the naïve confidence of a 15-year-old heavily made up to pass as 18, assured my mother, 'Don't you worry. … Most Yanks are absolute gentlemen, despite what people say about them.' [Which tended to be 'overpaid, over-sexed and over here'.] Mum retorted, 'Just as long as you know how to look after yourself and hop it when you need to.' Norma was unperturbed.

If the GIs brought novel delights to the young women of Britain, they did much for their younger brothers (and sisters) too. Many GIs were not long out of childhood themselves and they often found British children easier to get on with than their more reserved elders. And for the family men, time spent with youngsters could be some compensation for missing their own children thousands of miles away.

The currency of the relationship was chewing gum (with the Canadian troops, who had been stationed in Britain since soon after the outbreak of war, it was Sweet Caporal cigarette

Edward Ardizzone's painting 'West Country Manoeuvres: Camouflaged Bren Gun Carriers in a Lane'. Such scenes were common in many country lanes throughout southern England during the preparations for D-Day in June 1944.

cards). A Hertfordshire man who was seven when the GIs came to his home town recalls:

> constantly chasing them with cries of 'Got any gum, chum?' It must have been very irritating to say the least and I don't recall actually getting any gum, whatever that was, but my uncle told me that this was the correct way to greet Americans.

The 'gum chummers' as a Norfolk airbase nicknamed the clamouring children would be prepared to barter what the Americans wanted – jam jars, coat hangers, a trip to the fish and chip shop, even a date with their sister – for a stick of gum, or some US sweets. Chocolate Hershey bars, 'Babe Ruths' and hard candy (boiled sweets) such as 'Life Savers' were much coveted at a time of stringent rationing. An introduction to the great American subculture of the 'funnies' – comics featuring such characters as Superman, Captain Marvel, L'il Abner, Loony Toons, Red Ryder, the Katzenjammer Kids, and Bugs Bunny – often led to a lifetime addiction, as unfortunately did the habit some GIs had of bribing children to run errands not with sweets or comics but with cigarettes: 'such brands as Camel, Philip Morris, A1. … I remember having 21 cigarettes in one night … it's no wonder most kids smoked at nine or ten,' explains a man who as a small boy lived near a US camp in Pembrokeshire.

'Christmas, New Year, birthdays – any old birthday – Hallowe'en, Fourth of July, Thanksgiving, whatever celebrations the GIs cooked up, there was *always* – bombs or no bombs – a party for us kids,' relates a Norwich woman who lived surrounded by US air

Holidays at home

'Is your journey really necessary?' was a stern wartime inquisition originally posed to civil servants who had been evacuated with their ministries and wanted to go home for the weekend, but it soon appeared on every railway station in the country.

Train timetables were apt to be erratic and trains jam-packed because priority had to be given to moving troops and war matériel. The family car was jacked up on bricks in the garage since petrol for the private motorist was all but non-existent. So the government injunction to 'take

holidays at home' was more than a mere suggestion for thousands throughout the war, and children's horizons were further limited as parents valiantly tried to provide a good time in the back garden – if they had one.

Local authorities helped by laying on various entertainments, including concerts on bomb sites, dances in the park and Punch and Judy shows for the children.

bases in East Anglia. A Hertfordshire man who was evacuated to Middlesbrough as a child recalls how:

> At Christmas the Americans threw a superb party for the schoolchildren in the town hall. It was one of those grim public buildings of the time, with sandbags all around the lower ground floor. The [GIs] had decorated the interior with lots of flags – Stars and Stripes and Union Jacks together with tinsel and paper chains. ... They served an immense amount of food ... cakes, jellies and blancmange. ... We were all given a present from 'Santa', who had an American accent. I had a box of cardboard infantrymen. They had Stars and Stripes stickers and my hosts had to reassure me that they were on 'our side'.

For those children who were invited to 'Operation Reindeer' at Shipdham air base in Norfolk, 'coming into the huge hangar was like coming into Aladdin's Cave ... with coloured lights, streamers, silver bells and a Christmas tree reaching up to the skies'. Such trees would often be festooned with 'window' – the thin strips of metallic foil thrown out of aircraft to confuse German radar during a raid.

> There were sacks of sweets, stacks of sweets everywhere, and every now and then a great shower of sweets would be thrown into the air and the children, scrambling and screaming with delight, tumbled into an exuberant mass for a fistful of this treasure.

American wartime chewing gum.

173

The GIs would have saved up their sweet rations for weeks to provide this feast, and spent many evenings making toys, collecting money so they could buy whatever they could find in the shops, and writing home for small toys to be sent for the high point of the party: the arrival of Santa Claus. Usually he came by jeep, but at Shipdham:

> A droning was heard in the sky. ... Nearer and nearer it came. It was silver and 'snow' covered ... a Piper Cub plane. ... The propeller slowed and stopped and sure enough there he was. Father Christmas, with a red robe and white beard and a big bulging sack stepped from the plane.

On one occasion at the base he arrived in a huge US Flying Fortress bomber that taxied along the runway and children scrambled in to help Santa out of his 'sledge'.

GIs' generosity to British children extended to evacuees and those whose fathers had been killed or taken prisoner of war. The American Red Cross and the US forces newspaper *Stars and Stripes* jointly started an orphan fund. Each unit that collected £100 could 'adopt' a child who had lost one or both parents as a 'mascot' for a year. They could specify their requirements: 'a blue-eyed blonde girl' or 'a red-headed boy, no older than five'. The children – there were nearly 600 of them – would be sent sweets, toys and new clothes by their benefactors, and as well as being taken on trips and entertained, they would often visit the units that had 'adopted' them, and even be dressed in specially made US 'uniforms' for the occasion.

But though time spent with children might be delightful for the youngsters and while away the days for the GIs, it was coming to an end. By May 1944 there were over 1.5 million US troops in Britain. The reason they had come was to prepare for the invasion of Europe, Operation 'Overlord'. The south-west of England, from where the GIs (who would be fighting alongside but separately from Canadian and British troops) would set off, had become an arsenal. Planes and gliders stood, wingtips touching; tanks and lorries lined the roads; and bombs, weapons, ammunition and other supplies were crammed into any available space – waiting. The soldiers had been training for months, and beaches that were as similar as possible to the ones the men would encounter on the 'far shore' were requisitioned for training. Many of those who had been evacuated to Devon and Cornwall had to move out to make way for the troops. But not all.

King's School, Canterbury, had been evacuated to Cornwall in 1940 when raids over the city had become heavy. The boys were billeted in a variety of houses and hotels around St Austell, and on their walks along the cliffs and scrambles down to the coves and beaches, they found that they had a unique view of the Americans training. Brian Arnold, then a pupil at the school, recalls that:

> The Americans used to stack all their ammunition on either side of the road. You'd walk down the road and you were just walking through an ammunition corridor of explosives of all sorts. You'd just lean down and pick it up. It was as easy as that. We'd pick up blocks of gelignite which looked like packets of margarine, but luckily without detonators; there were shells of every calibre, anti-aircraft shells, and

174

Six-year-old Imogen Matthews drew this picture of the SS Samaria, the ship that took her, her mother, brother and sister to safety in the United States in June 1940. Her father, Edgar, was left in England and the number of small figures calling 'Daddy' is a reminder that the Matthews children were not alone in experiencing such wartime separation.

quite a lot of this stuff found its way into school. … One day we had a search at school in cupboards and things and we amassed quite a considerable pile of weaponry … dynamite, shells, mortars, hand grenades, small arms, these were all stacked – for safekeeping I suppose – under the bed of the school chaplain – a man of considerable girth who we always called 'the tank'.

The whole area was guarded, but there just weren't enough guards. We used to have a whale of a time driving amphibious vehicles out to sea, and really enjoying ourselves knocking bottles off the top of barbed-wire entanglements with American carbines. We saw the GIs practicing with these DUKWs all the time – they're a cross between a land vehicle and a boat, in fact they are rather better in water. But you had to remember to take the bungs out of the bottom when you got on land to let the water out, and it was rather important to remember to put them back in before you went back in the sea. … [One day] an American soldier was showing off. … He dashed into the sea and sank straight to the bottom instead of gliding across the surface [because he'd forgotten to replace the bungs]. It caused an enormous amount of mirth amongst us boys I'm afraid to say. He was okay, but they had to spend half a day fishing the DUKW off the bottom of the sea with a crane.

General Sir Bernard Montgomery, who was Commander of the Allied Land Forces, toured the country in the late spring of 1944 giving pep talks to the troops who would be going over to France. But he also made a point of visiting schools to talk to the JTCs [Junior Training Corps, formerly the OTC]. When he visited King's School he began his

175

'The Snowball Fight'. An evacuee from Farrance Street School, Limehouse, depicts life in the English countryside in winter.

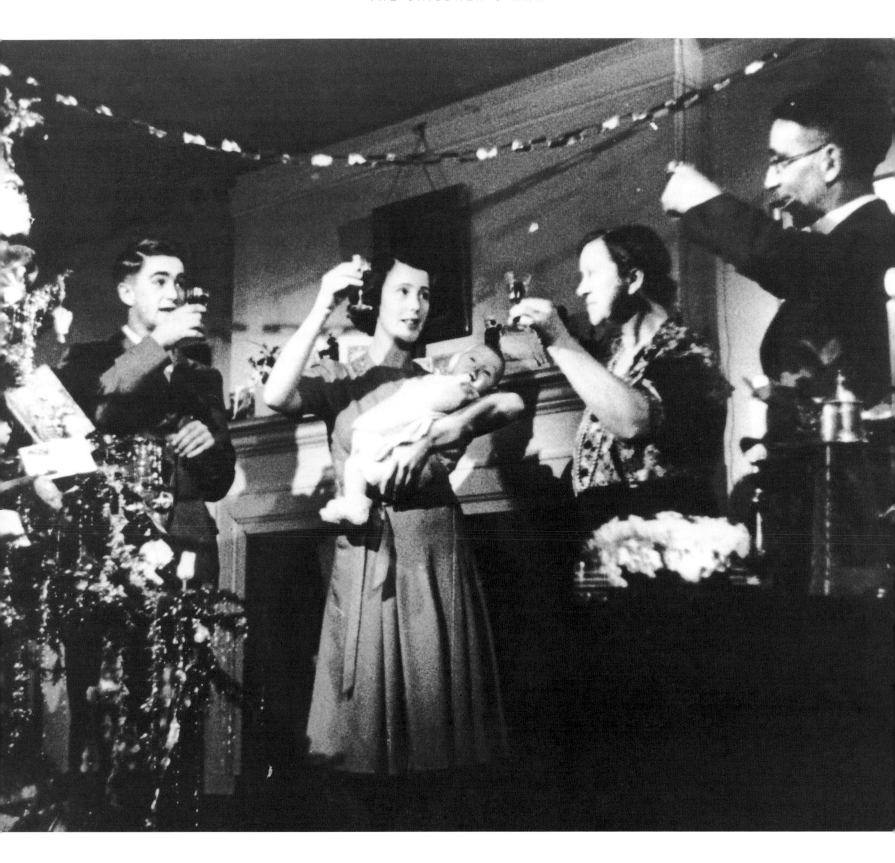

speech to the assembled boys by saying, 'I expect that everybody in this chapel here this morning would like me to tell you when the Second Front is going to start.' The opening of a Second Front – the Eastern Front with Russia was the first – was eagerly anticipated but top secret, and a great deal of Allied effort went into deceiving the Germans about exactly where and when the invasion would take place.

[We] all got very excited and he said 'Right, I'll tell you before I leave this hall.' And at the end of his lecture he said that the Second Front had already started, that the North Africa campaign was all part of a second front, and a landing in Europe wouldn't be the start. … We were quite disappointed. … We'd really thought he was going to let us boys in on a secret no one else knew.

But when the invasion did start, everyone knew it was D-Day. In early June St Austell 'was suddenly empty,' recalled a King's School pupil. 'The Americans in jeeps with white stars on and a special device in front of the windscreen to cut the piano wires the Germans stretch across the road, they suddenly all went. And the DUKWs disappeared like a vanished breed.'

A 16-year-old girl living on the Hampshire coast:

heard a rumour on 5 June that there were 'a lot of ships in the bay, so my mother and I went to the top of the cliffs between Boscombe and Bournemouth. I will never forget the sight that met our eyes: the bay was filled with ships of all sizes packed so tightly together that there was no sea visible between them. It was a clear, peaceful evening and I remember my mother saying, 'We're sure to be bombed tonight – the Germans couldn't miss such a target.' But there was no raid that night. Next day at lunchtime I decided to cycle home along the cliff road … but this time there was nothing to see but an empty bay. There was not one single ship in sight. … As I propped my bike against the wall at home, my mother called from the kitchen door. 'It's D-Day. We've landed in France. The invasion has started.'

Left: A still from Humphrey Jennings's slightly mawkish film A Diary for Timothy (1946). It was ostensibly made to show 'Timothy', who was born towards the end of the war, what it had all been about. E. M. Forster wrote the script which was narrated by Michael Redgrave.

Austerity continuing: a child's toy pram made by a demobbed soldier.

177

7

'It's peace at last'

Children gather round a Salvation Army mobile canteen after a V1 incident has destroyed several houses in Wandsworth, south-west London, in June 1944.

Back in September 1939 everyone had expected hostilities to start immediately war was declared, but apart from the war at sea it was eight months before Britain was threatened. Now that the long-planned Second Front had opened and Allied troops had established a foothold in France, everyone expected that the war would soon be over. It wasn't.

Eleven-year-old Robert Edom had recently been finding:

'life just incredibly dull, like Stowmarket on a Sunday. Then it all started up again. There was a dreadful night with sudden inexplicable explosions. Rumour had it that several planes packed with bombs had crashed. Then all was revealed. It was the dreaded doodlebugs. West Wickham [in Kent] got more than its fair share of these pilotless planes. Although [they] aimed at London, the … Krauts kept getting their sums wrong and they were dropping short. They came over in droves throughout the day. … These things rasped their way across the sky, stopped suddenly and then dived to earth. They made a hell of a bang and did my nervous twitch no good at all.'

The 'flying bomb' or V1 (standing for *Vergeltungswaffe Ein* or Revenge Weapon number one) was Germany's deadly secret weapon. The 25-foot-long, cigar-shaped missile flew without a pilot on a pre-set course for a pre-set distance up to around 140 miles. When it reached its destination, the circuit closed down and it plunged to earth in an 'eerie silence'. The first V1 to reach London fell in Bow in east London on the night of 13 June 1944, killing six people, including an eight-month-old baby, and seriously injuring 30. Over the next three months flying bombs came over night and day. By the end of June 231 children under 16 had been killed, and on 6 July, a month after D-Day, Churchill announced that 'up to 6 a.m. today 2,752 people have been killed by flying bombs and 8,000 have been detained in hospital.' On 30 June a children's residential nursery in an isolated part of the Kent countryside only a mile from Churchill's country home Chartwell, where very young London children had been evacuated, had been hit and the building collapsed on the sleeping infants. When the rescue parties arrived they found 'the garden a shambles of twisted metal cots, baby shoes, sheets and small blue blankets ... prams, a broken rocking horse, toys'. Twenty-two of the 30 children, all under five, were killed that night. The *News Chronicle* reported how:

> One by one, the tiny victims were recovered. A dark-haired baby boy in a blue knitted bed jacket – a fair-haired girl in pink – others just as they had been dressed and tucked in for the night. They were identified by the little labels tied to their ankles.

A woman living on the Isle of Wight with her two-and-a-half-year-old son felt the renewed attacks very deeply:

> From 9 o'clock until six or seven next morning we lie curled up in a cupboard under the stairs. When this house was built, close on a hundred years ago, they designed this huge cupboard running the whole length under the stairs to hold brooms and brushes ... never dreaming that in this year of our Lord 1944 it would contain a drop-side cot, four chairs, a small table, gas masks, torches, first-aid equipment, spades, hatchets and pickaxes (in case we have a chance to dig ourselves out), water and chocolate, and three or four adults and a baby, while outside the guns blaze, the searchlights sweep the night sky and the damned 'doodlebugs' roar across the garden.

179

In one of the most resonant images of the Second World War, a warden holds a terrified child who had just been rescued by a fireman from a house hit by a V1 flying bomb in southern England on 23 June 1944.

Children sitting on the edge of a bomb crater after a V1 flying bomb incident in Peckham, south-east London, in August 1944. The cups of tea have been supplied to them by one of the mobile canteens that always arrived to offer food and drink to those affected by such a disaster.

For the third time in five years, a dismal stream of evacuees from the capital started. On 5 July 1944, the first parties of homeless mothers and their children were evacuated from London and those parts of the Home Counties around the metropolis that the 'doodlebugs' (named after an insect found around the Mississippi) or buzz-bombs had again turned into 'bomb alley'. Trains leaving London termini were crammed with people wanting to get away, and suitable billets were harder to find than ever. By September, a combination of the 'priority classes' (mothers with infants under five, school-age children, expectant mothers and the aged and infirm) and those who had taken advantage of the 'assisted passage' provision (which provided free travel vouchers and billeting certificates which entitled the evacuees to a weekly allowance, though they had to find their own accommodation) totalled over a million. Even more people had just packed and gone as fast as they could to wherever they could. Many areas that had previously been classified as reception or neutral areas were now danger zones, and evacuees fanned out to the West Country, the Midlands and the north of England. By 7 September, the exodus had dwindled to a trickle and the scheme was suspended. The next day the second of Germany's deadly 'secret weapons' arrived.

Ronald McGill was playing cricket on Barnes Common on 8 September 1944 when:

The first ever V2 came down at Chiswick, which was our sports ground. And we were within a mile of there when that first V2 rocket fell. … When Dad came in

Victory

These two small girls were photographed by an anonymous US photographer on VE Day, 8 May 1945, in the rubble of some bombed-out houses in London. In the excitement, the girl on the right might have her flag mounted upside down, but her enthusiasm for victory is palpable.

The photograph was on display as part of a VE Day exhibition at the Imperial War Museum in 1995, and as a result the location was identified as being Henley Street, Battersea, in south London. Mrs Patricia Garcia (neé Lebby) also identified the flag-waver as her older sister, four-year-old Jeannie Lebby, and the child on the left as two-year-old Maureen Scholes. Tragically, having survived the war, Jeannie Lebby died soon afterwards of meningitis.

A cup showing the Allied 'Big Three', Stalin, Churchill and Roosevelt, 'United for Victory.'

Right: VE Day 8 May 1945. Celebrating crowds throng into Fleet Street as ticker tape is thrown from newspaper office windows.

182

the evening I said 'That was a new German thing, that noise.' And he said 'No it wasn't, it was probably a gas mains that blew up,' which was the official line for several weeks. [Ronald was unconvinced.] 'There was too many soldiers and police, it's something to do with Germany.' And he wouldn't believe me, but afterwards it turned out that it had been the first V2 rocket – just a mile away.

The V2, which was larger and heavier than its predecessor, was launched from sites within Germany and occupied Holland, since by then all of France was in Allied hands and the armies were advancing into Belgium. A news blackout was imposed for several weeks despite the obvious fact that people knew that a weapon of a different order was falling among them. Although fewer V2s fell, their impact was even more devastating. A single rocket could cause a crater 50 feet wide and 10 feet deep and demolish a whole street of houses, with the impact reverberating up to a quarter of a mile away. There could be no effective warning: all that would be heard was a tremendous thunderclap as the rocket plunged to earth. The worst V2 incident came on 25 November 1944, when one fell on a crowded Woolworth's store in New Cross, south-east London. 160 people were killed and 108 seriously injured. Two off-duty women railway carriage cleaners had taken their babies in their prams into Woolworth's for a cup of tea. No trace of either mothers or infants was ever found.

But in fact, as Barbara Roose noted, 'the war was drawing to an end.' The 'dimout', a dilute version of the blackout, had been gradually spreading since September 1944, though it was not until 24 April 1945 that the blackout was finally abolished, except for a five-mile coastal strip that remained dark until the war ended. 'The sight of the street lights going on and the round ball of revolving light on the top of the Coliseum glittering into our flat was unbelievable' after all those years of gloom and blackout, she wrote. The last civilian death as a result of enemy action occurred on 27 March 1945. But for the Roose family 'the thought that was uppermost in the minds of all three of us was [their father who was still abroad in the army]. Thank God that dad was still alive and hadn't been killed.'

Steve Turrell's parents were divorced and his father was doing war work. When the children's grandmother died and their father could no longer find anyone to look after his children, Steve and his sister were sent to a convent in Walthamstow to be cared for by nuns. The children were in school when news came that the German forces had surrendered.

A boy burst into the class shouting that the ice cream factory down the road was giving away free ice cream, one to each child. We all rushed out of the classroom and down the road with the teacher shouting out of the window, 'Come back here at once.' When we got there the queue seemed a mile long, but we waited and got our ice cream in a paper wrapper.

Later that evening the BBC interrupted a piano recital to announce that: 'Tuesday [8 May 1945] will be treated as Victory in Europe Day, and will be regarded as a holiday.'

In response to the cheers of the crowds on VE Day the royal family appeared on the balcony of Buckingham Palace – again and again. Princess Elizabeth (left) wears her ATS uniform. Later she and Princess Margaret Rose were allowed to mingle incognito with the celebrating crowds for a short time.

Lelia Faithful's painting 'VE Day Celebrations outside Buckingham Palace.'

On Marian's fourth birthday after the last few days of confusion, she and I [her mother, Verily Anderson] listened to the wireless announcement of the unconditional surrender of the German armed forces. 'Marian,' I said. 'You must remember this all your life. It's history.' But the reception was poor; and I could see that she would forget at once any word she happened to hear.

Michael Mason had been evacuated at the age of seven on 1 September 1939 from his school near the British Museum to the small village of Ashwell in Hertfordshire. In May 1945 he was still there, aged nearly 13. On VE Day:

[I] caught the early bus to Hitchin and from there to London. I wanted to spend the day with my mum and dad.

The scenes in the capital were incredible. It was one huge celebration. A tremendous wave of pent-up feelings had broken loose. People sang and danced, waved flags, climbed lamp-posts and blew whistles. The streets were crammed with joyful revellers, including the Mason family. We wandered down Tottenham Court Road, caught up in the surging mass of people, slowly making our way towards Trafalgar Square. The crowds were overwhelming, but good-natured. In Whitehall we called for 'Winnie' (Winston Churchill), and when he appeared an enormous cheer erupted.

Slowly we made our way down the Mall to Buckingham Palace, where we stood singing and calling for the King and Queen. Eventually they came out on the balcony, to be greeted with a huge roar of emotion and love from the gathering of happy people.

They returned to the balcony many times, and on each occasion a great cheer went up.

We ended up on the Embankment in the late evening to witness a huge firework display, the first I had seen for six years. It was a glorious climax to an unforgettable day.

'You'll remember this all your life.' A father gives his small daughter a potentially hazardous ride past Buckingham Palace on VE Day – much to the consternation of onlookers.

185

As soon as he heard the announcement, Ronald McGill decided that he and some friends would spend VE Day fishing in the ponds in Richmond Park. But his parents thought otherwise:

'Oh no you're not,' they said. 'You're coming with us to Buckingham Palace.'
'But I don't want to go to Buckingham Palace, I want to go fishing.'
And we had a terrible row because my friends went off and I had to go with my mum and dad on the Southern Railway to Vauxhall, walk up from there to Buckingham Palace and stand there with the rest of them cheering the King and Queen – while my heart was in Richmond Park fishing. But in the end I was glad I was there of course. It was a fabulous day really. It was the right thing to do. But I think that I really only realised that it was peace when my dad brought home some bananas. I'd never eaten a banana, and that was when I realised what war and peace was all about. … It was going to be a different world. Later that year I went on holiday, my first real holiday. I went away with some other boys cycling on the Isle of Wight and then I knew it really was peace. A different world.

Mary Whiteman thought that relief rather than jubilation was the dominant feeling on 8 May. 'People were just so tired. The war had gone on so long. In my neighbourhood [in Essex] it was only the Americans who made any noise with fireworks and dancing

A child's home-made 'Victory' waistcoat.

and things.' Mrs Whiteman's baby was due on 8 May and she 'kept praying that he wouldn't be born on VE Day or I'd have felt I should have called him Victor or Monty or something like that. But luckily he was born two days later.'

Peter Holloway and his brother Stanley were still evacuated in Devon:

> The full import of events didn't dawn on [us] immediately. Mr and Mrs Hagley [the boys' wartime foster parents] took us to a grand Victory parade in Lynton where a Spitfire was on display and the representatives of the armed forces marched past. I remember one airman being out of step and even at my age I felt very sorry for him. The children queued up for the great honour of sitting in the Spitfire and to my great surprise the cockpit was small even for a child. My brother Stanley completely filled the available space so I assumed all Spitfire pilots were chosen for their diminutive size.

In September 1941 King's Warren school had been evacuated from south London to Maidstone and then Bedford, and it was there that Dorothy King saw VE Day.

> We met for Assembly after which we were dismissed for two days' holiday! HV and I cycled along feeling very happy. It was warm and sunny, nearly every house was decorated with flags and pennants, children were riding about with little Union Jacks attached to their bikes and everyone was sauntering about on holiday. There has, in fact, been a bank holiday atmosphere about today. No one is at work and everyone is wearing their best clothes.

In many 'suburban and provincial celebrations', it was less a question of crowds thronging the streets several deep, hokey-cokeying, and singing; rather:

> 'the outstanding features, and the ones that gave the most pleasure, were bonfires, street parties and fireworks, activities meant in the first place for children … though in most places adults themselves were jolted into excitement and joined in.'

In one unnamed town, a Mass-Observation correspondent reported that:

> 'Everybody participated in the making of Hitler. One lady gave the jacket, another the trousers and so on until Hitler's rig-out was assured. … The Chief Fire Watcher in

Dancing in the streets to celebrate the end of war in Europe. The scene at the Pantiles, Tunbridge Wells, on VE Day.

the road made the face, and some of the boys fitted up the gallows, but one of the men erected it for them. ... One of the men suggested they burn Goering [commander of the Luftwaffe] too, and he volunteered to make him, complete with medals and two Iron Crosses and he was seated in a chair at the feet of Hitler. Lying nearby was a battered doll, face and body daubed with red paint as a reminder of the misery Hitler ... had brought to humanity. Two Union Jacks and bunting hung from the wooden posts in front of the bombed site.

From about 7 o'clock onwards children collected round, watching the proceedings to make sure that they weren't going to miss anything despite the fact that the proceedings weren't billed to start until 9.30 p.m. ... In front of the bonfire two planks supported by bricks were marked RESERVED SEATS – and some were labelled FOR STOKERS ONLY.

At 9.15 p.m. a gramophone started to play light music and by this time there must have been around 30 children and 20 adults, standing about in the road watching the goings-on ... [At] 9.30 p.m. the Chief Fire Watcher was invited to light the bonfire. One of the boys handed him a long pole, at the end of which was a rag soaked in paraffin. Immediately the bonfire was lit, a cheer went up. Hitler started to burn too quickly and [in response to] cries of "Don't let him end up so soon, let him linger," boys promptly doused him with the hose in order to prolong the burning. ... Children danced round the bonfire yelling at the tops of their voices. Flares were let off and with each bang the children screamed with fright.

At 9.40 p.m. a piano was carried into the roadway and a lady played popular songs, "Roll Out the Barrel", "Tipperary", "Daisy, Daisy, Give Me Your Answer Do", "Knees UP Mother Brown". ... Four young girls (aged about 15) are singing and doing the "Lambeth Walk" in the middle of the road. No one appears to notice them. A lot of girls are walking along in groups and smoking cigarettes. This is not often seen in the streets round here – part of the celebrations perhaps? ...

Grown-ups and children joined hands round the bonfire and sang all together and by now there must have been at least 150 people. Neighbours standing in small groups outside their garden gates watching joined in the singing too. At about 11 p.m. the smaller children left, but the older boys were very reluctant to

Children in paper hats tuck into the feast that their mothers prepared from goodies they had been saving up for months – even years. 'VE Street Party', painting by Edwin La Dell.

187

Right: Children stand watching a victory bonfire burning on the night of VE Day, 8 May 1945.

Chelsea children celebrate the coming of peace to Europe with a street party. This was held in July 1945 – a little more than a month before the war with Japan was over too, and the world was at peace … for a time.

go, despite repeated calls of 'Come on, you've got to go to bed – you'll never get up in time for school'. By about 11.30 p.m. the crowd had all dispersed.'

Babara Roose recalls the atmosphere as VE Day approached.

A street party, that's what we want, was the thought of everyone in 'the Bury'. As the last days and weeks of the war dragged by, the women got together. Every family saved a few precious points from their rations to buy tinned and dried fruit for the great party. The 8th of May saw the end of hostilities [in Europe] and plans got under way for the party.

Bunting and flags were already hanging from every available window. The trestle tables stretched for about 60 feet and they were borrowed from our friends the Canadian soldiers in St Peter's Hospital.

Every family had their chores. Some of the ladies made sandwiches, some jellies and blancmange, others cakes and pastries with one huge, square, iced Victory cake.

We were all hopping with excitement and for once all too willing to help and run errands. Sheets appeared on the tables for tablecloths and all the children brought their own cup, plate and spoon and not forgetting a chair.

I had a new ribbon for my hair … while Geoff's hair was smarmed down with Brylcreem. At 5 o'clock sharp the festivities began. We tucked into as much as we could eat … while the grown-ups, in high spirits, stood around us chattering and drinking tea. The staff from the [gentleman's outfitters] Moss Bros, whose back entrance led into our yard, traipsed out as the shop closed to join in the fun.

The highlight of the party was the ceremonial cutting of the cake. There wasn't any doubt who we wanted for this honour, that was Vic Oliver [the entertainer and one-time son-in-law of Winston Churchill]. He [had appeared] in *Black Velvet* at the Coliseum [near 'the Bury' in Covent Garden] and he grandly came along. Most of us knew him to shout 'Hello' to and when he stood in our shabby yard, crowded with happy faces, he was one of us. … After that, the tables were swiftly cleared. Everybody took their own dirty crocks, chairs and tablecloth and the ding-dong party began in earnest. The beer and orange juice flowed. An upright piano appeared from one of the flats into the yard. We sang and danced the night away and nobody was sent to bed early. Lights shone from the windows in a lovely carefree way with no thought of the blackout ever again.

An Oxfordshire village held a VE Day party too:

> We had a really magnificent tea for the children – jam tarts with a V sign in chocolate being the great delicacies. The children marched along singing and waving flags. … They looked so pretty. There were at least 50 of them. Luckily there was just enough food. We played games and there were 6d stamps for prizes. … We kept looking at them enjoying themselves and thinking peace has really come at last after all these years of strain and tension. … A wonderful, wonderful feeling to know that after more than five and a half years all our splendid young men are not killing people or getting killed. Peace really has begun to come slowly into our hearts.

189

But peace had only come to Europe. In the Far East the war continued. 'I wonder how people have the heart to rejoice, knowing what misery people have had and are still having with the Japanese war. I don't feel like rejoicing. It doesn't feel like a day of joy for me,' a woman told a Mass-Observation reporter. 'Many people in Eton and Windsor were annoyed by the victory celebrations because their men in the Oxford and Bucks [Oxfordshire and Buckinghamshire Light Infantry] are still fighting in Burma – though this didn't deter the majority one little bit,' another women said. Others had heard the news and seen on the newsreel pictures the British liberation of the concentration camp at Belsen. The knowledge of how many Jews – including children and young people – had perished there, leaving deracinated orphans over all Europe, struck another hollow note. *The Observer* concluded:

> The [people] knew the war was not really over and they felt it was really too early to celebrate, but the European war was finished … and people were expected to celebrate and there was at last an opportunity for grown-ups and children to really enjoy themselves at last. … Most people's behaviour was an effort to strike some sort of a balance between their impulses, and many other feelings which are too deep for expression, or even awareness.

The end of the war in Japan finally came on 14 August 1945 when Japan surrendered

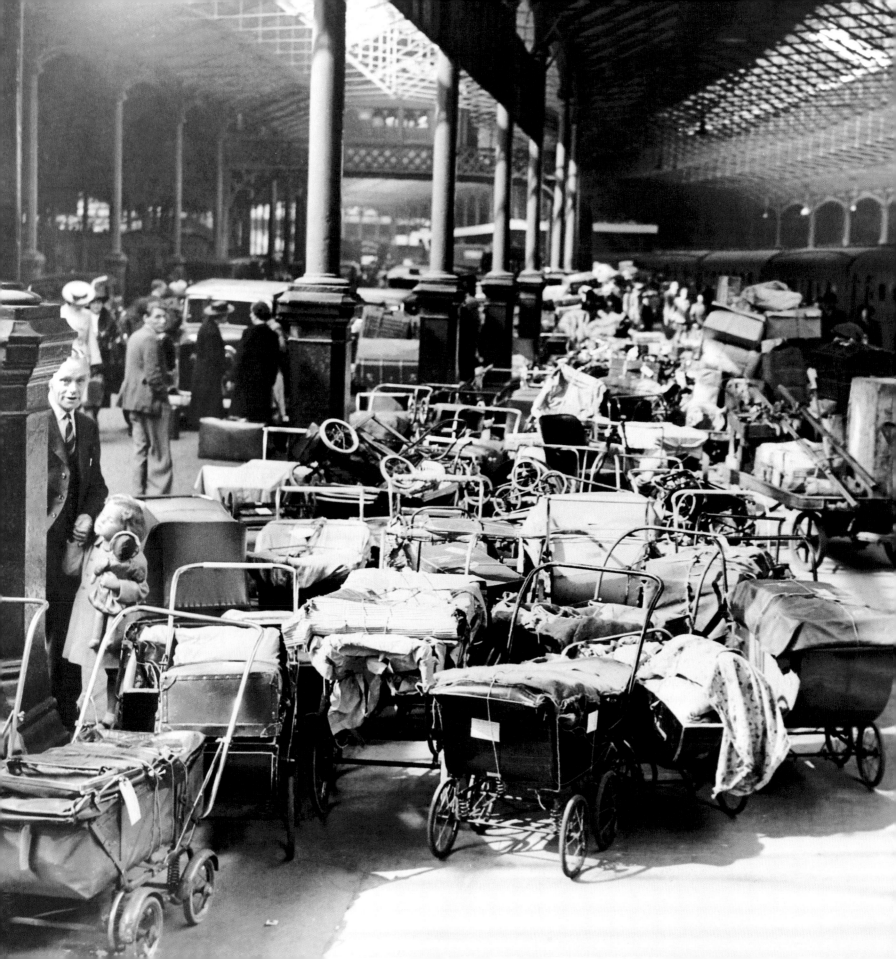

after the Americans dropped atomic bombs on Hiroshima and Nagasaki, immediately killing over 150,000. 'There was a world of difference between VE Day and VJ Day' on 15 August for a Scottish woman who 'wanted to rejoice but there is no way of doing so.'

Albany Road School had come back to Camberwell from Weymouth in May 1942. Other schools, finding their arrangements too unsatisfactory in the reception areas, or that too many of their pupils had returned leaving but a skeleton school behind, upped sticks and returned too. Mary Datchelor School was one that was split; when the school opened for the autumn term in September 1944, 260 girls remained in Llanelli while over 200 were being taught in London 'as the flying bombs fell', though on occasion 'new children joined us [in Wales] and also parents, who had been bombed out'.

At the beginning of the summer term of 1945, Dr Brock:

> heard that the LCC was instructing secondary schools to remain in the reception area until the end of term; but our conditions for doing examinations were so difficult that we made a special appeal to be allowed home before the examinations began.

VE Day came and went, but on 11 May the headmistress was 'able to tell the School that we were going home on May 28th. I shall never forget their reception of the news and the cheers that welcomed me when I announced it.' And home the pupils and teachers went, to reoccupy a school building that had been requisitioned by the Metropolitan Gas Board for the duration.

Parents who had made arrangements to send their children away privately without government help could, of course, bring them back when they wanted, but as there had been official government schemes to get children away, so there were to bring them back. Evacuees started to return to Merseyside from North Wales in late November 1944, followed by those returning to Scotland and the Midlands. Flying bombs and rockets meant that London was still not considered safe, and the north-east (Hull in particular) was still suffering from conventional raids, but on 2 May 1945 the London Return Plan was put into effect. In the middle of May all London schools closed for a fortnight so that the teachers could check out what sort of conditions the children would be returning to. Some homes were manifestly unsuitable: they might have been made uninhabitable as a result of enemy action, with the family broken up and living in accommodation that was not suitable for a child, or parents might still be engaged in war work and not able to care for their children. One – or both – parents might have been killed, or for some other reason be unable – or unwilling – to care for their offspring. In such cases the evacuees would remain in their foster homes until something could be sorted out. The evacuees started coming back on special trains in early June, but by August 76,000 children still remained in the reception areas.

Left: The return (I). Prams arrive at Euston station in advance of their evacuee occupants.

The return (II). Villagers say goodbye to some of the evacuees who have been living with them for much of the war.

191

192

The return (III). 'Make sure you come and see us again soon'. A village turns out to wave off its returning evacuees.

This was more than had been brought home, usually because of housing or other social problems in their home towns or cities.

'The idea of going back to London had been uppermost in our minds at the beginning of the war: London after all was home,' a home Peter and Stanley Holloway had initially been reluctant to leave:

But with the passing of the seasons and the years, home had inevitably become Parracombe and Bodley Cottage [in Devon]. We knew about country life, about horses and farming, about the multiplicity of wildlife that abounded in the valley. London was for me a word which had come to represent life elsewhere. For Stanley, memories of London must have been more firmly established. He could remember people and places, relatives and neighbours, but to me it was a foreign land. One late autumn morning, Mr and Mrs Hagley informed us that we were going back to our parents in London. Lillian Hagley tried to sound matter-of-fact and Bill sat by the fireside smoking his pipe. . . .

The full impact of leaving came by small degrees. A number of villagers were standing by the [coal] lorry [that was to take them to Barnstaple station] when we

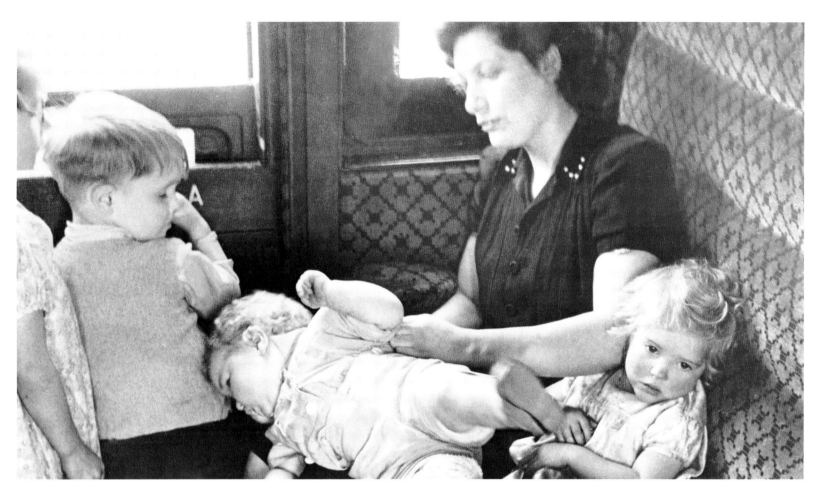

193

climbed into the cab. … We carried small cases and wore new blue raincoats. Mrs Leeworthy gave us chocolate and Granny Hoyles kissed us goodbye. We promised faithfully to write as soon as we could and waved vigorously as George backed his lorry past the blacksmith's shop opposite the Fox and Goose. … We waved goodbye and our last view of the village was through the rear window as we struggled in second gear up one of the steepest hills in Devon. Nobody spoke much as we travelled the 14 miles to Barnstaple. … In the hour that we waited for the train Mrs Hagley tried to be cheerful and spoke of life in our new schools and the big city. Stanley was to go to South East London Technical College since he had shown an aptitude for technical education. My future was somewhat more in doubt and depended on a strange test called the 'scholarship' which I would face soon after arrival. At last the train arrived. … Mr Hagley put his pipe aside long enough to say 'Now don't you miss that there connection at Exeter,' but already tears were running down his cheeks. Lillie gave up all pretence at formality and we all hugged each other and wept uncontrollably.

We waved from the carriage window until they were no more than dots on the platform, then slumped dejectedly in the corner of the carriage. … We had to

The return (IV). A tired mother and her young children on the train home from their evacuation experience.

8th June, 1946

To-day, as we celebrate victory, I send this personal message to you and all other boys and girls at school. For you have shared in the hardships and dangers of a total war and you have shared no less in the triumph of the Allied Nations.

I know you will always feel proud to belong to a country which was capable of such supreme effort; proud, too, of parents and elder brothers and sisters who by their courage, endurance and enterprise brought victory. May these qualities be yours as you grow up and join in the common effort to establish among the nations of the world unity and peace.

George R.I.

194

change platforms at Exeter and my first surprise was to see people passing each other as if they were invisible. In Parracombe nobody passed anybody without a nod or a smile. … Stanley said … that people were like that in big cities. There were so many people, he confided, that they simply ignored each other. …

The express train steamed into the platform and we joined a crowded train taking a large number of servicemen back to London. We were ignored as we jammed into a corner of the carriage and most of those around us wanted to sleep or smoke. … One of the soldiers kept talking about 'when we get to the smoke', and … Stanley and I were baffled at what this meant. … Later I was learn that this was the term, universally used by servicemen, for London, and not without reason. As we reached the outskirts of the metropolis the sunlight disappeared behind a curtain of yellow fog. … Gradually the train shunted and jerked its way into Waterloo station. … We hurried nervously towards the ticket barrier. … Everywhere seemed to be covered in black dust and dirt swirling around amidst the steam and billowing fog. A small figure stood beside the uniformed ticket collector at the barrier, looking uncertainly in our direction. He was about five feet tall, and Stanley towered over him as we stiffly shook hands. He was my father and I didn't recognise him. …

On the bus … my father kept up a running commentary about the important places we were passing and the large bomb sites where the Luftwaffe had left their trade mark. … We disembarked at New Cross Gate and walked through a maze of back streets behind Millwall football ground. Large timbers met in a 'V' shape in the middle of the road and supported the houses threatening to collapse. We approached one of these in Erlam Road and a pale face peered out through the window. My mother came to the door and talked incessantly about having us back again. … My father said very little. Everything in the room was covered with a fine layer of dirt since the roof was only temporarily repaired. An incendiary bomb had come through the roof into the scullery, but had been put out before it could burn. The lighting came from a gas mantle that had been damaged and a small blue flame leaped spasmodically from a jagged hole. I noticed that my brother's face was covered in grime, as must have been my own. Not the clean red earth of Devon but the filth pouring from a million chimneys into the smoke pall overhanging London. At that moment I felt a nudge against my ankle and looking down I saw a large black and white bundle of fur. I picked up the cat and it nuzzled its head under my chin like a long-lost friend. It was a warming incident on the blackest of days.

Barbara Helical, returning after nearly six years as a 'seavacuee' in Australia, had an even worse homecoming:

I stood on Leeds station. There was a heavy mist swirling and everyone had gone. I'd passed this couple about three times. They didn't know that it was their daughter, and I didn't know it was my parents. I felt so lonely.

The *Liverpool Daily Post* described how a party of the 'first contingent of school children evacuated to Wales' on the outbreak of war had arrived back at Lime Street station singing:

> The words of the song sounded like a foreign language. Were the children little French, Dutch or Belgian refugees? They were Liverpool children all right, greeting their native city with a rendering of 'Calon Lân'. ... Many of them [have] been living in an area where English is hardly ever spoken and they can now speak Welsh as well as their mother tongue. A few of them have forgotten practically all the English they have ever learned!

The return (V). September 1945: A party of evacuees arrive at Southampton on board HMT Andes. When they went to Australia in 1940 they were children: now they are returning as young adults.

A child's autograph book.

Occasionally a foster parent would adopt – either formally or informally – a child who had been billeted with them. Marjorie Baker's older sister Margaret, who had been evacuated from Liverpool to the Welsh Borders, was taken in by a childless couple:

> They didn't have any children because they had married late in life so of course they didn't want to let her go, and they gave her things she couldn't have at home. When Mrs W. asked if she could adopt Margaret, my father thought she would have more opportunities and a better education, which she did. My mother never forgot her. I don't think she realised at the time that she'd never see her again.

Children who had left their parents when they were eight or nine would be 14 when it was time to come home: old enough to leave school. A number opted to stay in the country and find work there or, in the case of girls who were 16 in 1945 and had had romances with local boys, decided to marry their 'reception area' sweethearts and set up a new home.

But even those children who had eagerly looked forward to going home found that family life would never be quite the same again. Close on six years' separation had changed them; they had learned different ways and values, and readjustment was hard. Walter Hurst had 'been most anxious to return home but it took a long time to get used to being part of a normal family again and I never really managed to make a good relationship with my father.'

'Making a relationship with father' was not a problem confined to evacuees. Many fathers who had been serving in the army, navy or air force, or working away from home in war industries, could be total strangers to their children – particularly if they had been babies when their fathers went away. They might know their fathers only as a photograph they had dutifully kissed before they went to bed every night, and from stories their mother had told them, or snippets she had read out from letters.

Demobilisation – with a few exceptions – was prioritised by age and length of service. It was slower than anyone would have liked – a series of sit-down strikes at the slow pace flared up at RAF bases in India and the Middle East in January 1946 – but on the whole, given the complexities involved, the system worked well. But getting out of the forces was one thing. Getting back into civilian life was another. There was the demob suit to acquire, the gratuity to collect, a job to go back to – or find – and a family to get to know all over again.

Gwen Price's father went away in early 1941 when she was ten months old, and it was over four years before she saw him again:

> No one prepared me for our meeting. … We were at Reading station on this cold December day and all of a sudden this great big man picked me up and cuddled me! I screamed the place down and nothing my mother could say or do would induce me to go near him for quite a time. … It was very difficult. … I had mostly slept with my mother or grandmother during the war, and for this man to want to sleep with my mother made me feel very fed up and lost!

Vote for me ...

Ernest Bevin, the wartime Minister of Labour, canvassing for votes in Wandsworth during the 1945 election campaign.

The wartime coalition with Churchill at its helm came to an end on 23 May 1945. The Prime Minister had wanted to carry on until Japan was defeated but the Labour Party refused.

Polling day was 5 July but, as there were so many soldiers overseas whose votes had to be counted, the ballot boxes would not be opened until 26 July 1945.

The irony of the service vote was stark: at 18 they were considered old enough to fight and die for their country, but not to vote. They could not help select the government until they were 21.

The Conservatives appealed for voters to 'Let Him Finish the Job,' but when the votes were counted it was a landslide for Labour. The voters clearly preferred Labour's appeal to 'Face the Future,' particularly when it came to housing, and trusted them as the party most likely to implement Beveridge's plans for health and the welfare of children, though ironically Beveridge, a Liberal, lost his seat in the election.

198

Father's return

Re-introducing Father to the family, and vice versa.

By Pearl Binder

Josephine's airgraph

ONE of these days, maybe sooner than we dare hope, a sunburnt figure in uniform is going to come walking up the garden path, through the front door, and into our lives again.

For five years we have been making plans and building hopes for the future. We shall have our husband back, the children their daddy back. But don't let us delude ourselves into thinking we shall all carry straight on from where we left off. There is going to be a lot of adjustment to be done, and perhaps it might be as well to think over the difficulties now as well as the delights.

Five years is a long time and children forget quickly. My two-and-a-half-year-old baby Elizabeth certainly won't remember her daddy. She was one and a half when he went overseas. Daniel, who is now three and a half, *may*—I doubt it—though I am sure he is eager to persuade himself he does remember,

and will, therefore, be very ready to fling himself upon that man in khaki and claim him as his daddy. Of course Josephine, who is six, will remember. But just what will she remember? A mixture of wistful hopes and fantasy and the warm security of having two parents, even though one is absent. Once or twice, disguised as a sort of game, I have asked her to describe her daddy to me. This is the sort of thing she says: 'Tall and laughing, with funny eyebrows, and a beautiful crown on his shoulder.'

And my husband has only been away one year. Some fathers have been overseas for as long as four years or more. The mere toddler who kissed daddy good-bye will now be an assured schoolboy. And some of us have sturdy children whose daddies have never yet set eyes on them.

Nevertheless, it is my firm conviction

27

Peter Crane had been in a Japanese POW camp and there had been little news of him other than the odd postcard. When he finally came home his children:

> just stared at him, round-eyed … and when he kept saying, 'Don't do this' and 'Don't do that,' they said, 'Mum, who's that man that keeps coming in our house and staying all night?' I said 'It's your father.' 'Well, we don't like him – who is he? Tell him to go away.' And it seemed terrible to me that … they didn't like him … after all he'd been through.

Very young children could be even more confused: some could not bring themselves to honour their fathers with the name 'daddy' and addressed them for years as 'mister', while May Griffiths's two-year-old baby sister 'had never seen her daddy. His picture on the wall was her daddy and she insisted on kissing his picture good night for a considerable time rather than him. … We didn't appreciate how hard this was on my father.'

But for some children, the return of their father was all-important. For Barbara Roose:

> It was late summer 1945, the war was over, but to us, it wouldn't be over until Dad came home. … Other kids' dads had come back but there was no sign of our dad appearing from Italy. Mum grumbled, 'Just my luck, he's first away and last back.'
>
> I was sitting on a wall outside 'D' block looking on to the street. … The sun was comfortably warm as I swung my legs and hummed one of Deanna Durbin's songs. …
>
> The taxi stopped at the entrance to our yard. The iron gates that once stood there had been taken down years ago to help the war effort. I regarded the taxi with interest. Nobody in 'the Bury' owned a car and it was only on very special occasions that anyone came or went in a taxi. A soldier climbed out and paid the cabbie and dumped his knapsack and kitbag on the pavement. I stared at him and my heart started to race. He was a great big man. Was this man my dad? He didn't look much like the young soldier in the photograph on the mantelpiece and this man had a moustache. The soldier stood and stared at the buildings and the yard and didn't move. The spell was broken by Mrs Shambler who lived on the third floor of 'E' block. She was watching us and shouted down to me, 'Barbara, that's your dad.' I walked slowly up to him and said nervously, 'Dad, Dad?' 'Barbara?' He swept me up into his arms and gave me a kiss. His moustache tickled. For me the war was over.

8 Epilogue: The innocents

Wars may end in jubilant victory celebrations but no war produces any winners, and children were victims of the Second World War to an extent never known in previous conflicts. Probably around 55 million adults and children, military and civilian, died between 1939 and 1945, and many more later from the effects of war. In Britain's armed forces, 264,443 men and 624 women were killed; 3,596 of them were under 18 years of age, and 18 were only 14 years old. In the Merchant Navy and fishing fleets, 30,248 men were killed, and 1,206 members of the Home Guard died while on duty. Thousands of children were left to grow up without a father.

On the Home Front in Britain 60,595 civilians were killed (including Civil Defence personnel), again leaving thousands of children who had lost one or sometimes both parents, as well as grandparents, brothers and sisters and other relations and friends whose loss would diminish their lives for ever. Of that total, 7,736 children under 16 were killed by enemy action – approximately one death in every eight – and 7,662 were seriously wounded.

There can be no balance sheet for death. Every single death of a child is as shocking as the next. But the aggregate numbers can still be numbing. More than 1,200,000 Jewish children died in the Holocaust; indeed only 11 per cent of Jewish children living in Europe in 1939 survived the war. In Germany, 6 million children under the age of 16 were involved in the 'total war' as combatants and as civilians, and many of those can be counted among the over 3 million dead, wounded and missing of the German armed forces; nearly 4 million German civilians were killed. In the last desperate days of the battle for Berlin in 1945, members of the Hitler Youth, some of them as young as 12, fought the Red Army; only around 10 per cent of them survived. In the Warsaw Rising between August and October 1944, 20,000 children died, and 400,000 perished in the siege of Leningrad. In July 1943, 5,586 children were killed in the Allied raids on Hamburg. Japanese schoolchildren, most armed only with swords, fought US forces on Okinawa in April 1945. No one knows how many children were killed, died later – sometimes decades later – of their injuries, or were born malformed as the result of the bombing of Nagasaki and Hiroshima.

At the end of the war Poland had a million orphans; one Greek child in every eight had no parent left alive. A conservative estimate suggests that there were 30 million displaced persons wandering Europe in 1945, and a large number of these homeless refugees – probably around 13 million – were abandoned children.

To focus on Britain in the 'people's war': many children suffered the dangers and hardships of war with their parents, and many grew up with knowledge and anxieties beyond their years. In all, 1,655,710 children were evacuated under the official evacuation

A new Jerusalem?

If the Second World War had been a 'people's war' with equal sacrifices expected from all, and everyone (well, almost) pulling together to defeat the enemy, then what was needed was a 'people's peace' with a fairer distribution of rewards than there had been in the pre-war world. During the war the state had regulated almost every aspect of people's lives: what they ate, where they worked, what they could wear. But when peace came, what role would it play in building the new Jerusalem that everyone felt they had earned the right to look forward to?

The Beveridge Report seemed to point the way. Published in December 1942 it was an instant best-seller, shifting over 100,000 copies in the first month of publication. Though it was hardly revolutionary, the report promised a security net for all 'from the cradle to the grave' against the ravages of poverty caused by sickness or unemployment. There would be a state allowance for children, a national health service 'available to all members of the community ... without charge on treatment at any point' – which would be a great relief for those poor families who had not always been able to afford to call a doctor when a child lay sick – and the promise that the state would use its 'full powers to maintain employment and banish unemployment', the spectre that had haunted the 1930s for so many.

The Beveridge 'plan', as people were soon calling it, coupled with R. A. Butler's 1944 Education Act, really seemed to promise a brighter future for young people. The Act committed the government to raise the school-leaving age to 15 (which the Labour government did in 1947) and to replace the elementary schools with a tripartite system based on 'parity of esteem', whereby the more academic child would receive a grammar school education, there were technical schools for those so minded, and there were secondary moderns – well, they were really for the rest.

It never quite worked out like that: local authorities built few technical schools, and secondary moderns could have lamentably low expectations of their pupils' abilities. But taken in tandem, Butler and Beveridge did begin a courageous wartime attack on behalf of future generations on those 'five giants' that Beveridge had declared needed slaying on the road to a just society: 'Want, Disease, Ignorance, Squalor and Idleness.'

Above left: William Beveridge talking to evacuees.

Above right: Abram Games's poster of the future Britain was fighting for: the Welfare State.

Right: A healthy future. A post-war baby drinks Ministry of Health supplied orange juice.

R. V. Steed was the youngest person to be killed on active service in the Second World War. His ship hit a mine off North Africa and the 14-year-old galley boy was drowned. He is buried in Morocco.

202

scheme on 1 September 1939 and later exoduses (1,134,235 with their schools and 721,425 with their mothers). Many found the experience enjoyable. They settled down with kindly foster parents and enjoyed country life. Thousands did not; they suffered either cruelty, abuse or neglect, or simply a feeling of rejection and intense loneliness. Frequently the fragile bonds of family life were never properly re-established, and some children entered adulthood wary, withdrawn or aggressive, and not easily able to make secure relationships. Many children's education suffered grievously during the war from inadequate schooling, poor teaching and lack of resources, and this narrowed their life chances. The notion that country life unequivocally benefited children, that they grew stronger and healthier with 'good country fare', plenty of fresh air and knowledge of the 'real world' rather than mere book learning, has been exaggerated. As Dr Brock wryly observed, even though the experience in the country had succeeded in teaching one young London schoolchild that a cow is ' "a perishin' 'orse with handlebars" ... the study of the cow is no substitute for covering the General School syllabus.'

The upheavals of war also led to an increase in juvenile crime, and with the schools shut for much of the time, the lawless youth 'running wild' in the blitzed cities and causing havoc in the countryside was an unshakable image of the effects of war. On the outbreak of war, in order to clear accommodation for so-called 'enemy aliens', it had been decided that all Borstal boys and girls in approved schools or remand homes who had served at least six months of their sentence would be released. But of the 2,817 boys set free under the scheme, 50 per cent were back inside again by 1943, and 56 of the girls by 1946, which confirmed the opinion of some Chief Constables that such institutions offered little more than apprenticeship schemes for crime. Crime-reduction and rehabilitation schemes, inadequate in the pre-war years, were all but non-existent in wartime.

In the first year of the war the number of children under 14 found guilty of criminal offences rose by 41 per cent; for young persons aged between 14 and 17, the rise was 22 per cent, and for those between 17 and 21 around 5 per cent. The massive proliferation of indictable offences that wartime regulations had instigated, from black-out transgressions to 'profiteering' to petty looting, meant that police resources were vastly overstretched, and places of detention and correction all but overflowing. As a result many Chief Constables, aware how out of joint the times were, advised their men to caution young miscreants for relatively minor cases, rather than hauling them before the courts.

The finger was pointed at many causes for this rise in juvenile crime: the blackout gave effective cover for hooliganism, gambling and sexual licence; public shelters and unoccupied blitzed houses offered refuge for truants and runaways; and higher wages for adolescents – on average raised from £3 a week to £6 – gave them money to spend on drink and gambling (though it was odd that before the war it was the lack of money that had been blamed for delinquent behaviour, and anyway the sharpest rise in crime was among schoolchildren). But the most usual culprit was seen as family breakdown, lax parenting, the absence of a father or often even of a father figure when so many men were away, the rupture of the mother–child bond caused by evacuation, and the advent of the wartime 'latch-key kid' where the father might be in the forces and the mother at work for long hours on war production.

Children's wartime diet, though monotonous, was usually adequate, often because mothers denied themselves sufficient food so their children would flourish. But children's horizons were narrowed through lack of holidays and treats, and sometimes by the xenophobia that is a less-often talked-of curse of war, and their imagination was curbed through the unavailability of toys and books.

Yet, yet – many are the adults today who talk about their wartime childhood as a very happy time, one of excitement and freedom, and of self-reliance and looking out for others. The war, evacuation in particular, woke up the nation to the plight of underprivileged children: there might have been much prejudice about dirty, diseased and undisciplined urban urchins, but reports and surveys highlighted the appalling conditions in which many such children lived: the unacceptable city slums, the failure of the medical authorities to monitor the health of children adequately, the grim poverty in which such children were growing up, and the lack of support for their parents.

In 1939, 751 people had been found guilty of child cruelty or neglect; by 1944 this figure had doubled. This could be read as a damning indictment of people under stress in wartime; it obviously speaks to the fact that so many children were billeted with unvetted and sometimes unsuitable 'carers', but it can also be seen as evidence that more notice was taken of children's plight: that they were beginning to be seen as a charge on the nation's conscience, rather than the responsibility only of whoever was charged with their care.

That was one aspect of the great gains of war as far as children were concerned. Their needs and interests were increasingly put to the forefront of the government's agenda, whether it was ensuring their health with the provision of milk and other body-building foods and vitamins, or the recognition that the education system was failing so many children. Enshrined in the provisions of the 1944 Education Act was its emphasis on 'parity of esteem', and gradual acceptance that the socialisation of children from a young age was an important aspect of their development. With all this was a recognition that in the modern world the concept of community had changed for ever, and had to be reconstituted in the interests of the child.

None of these things represented an epiphany, none led to a new Jerusalem for the under-18s, but to a considerable extent children would figure prominently in any vision of the post-war future and would be beneficiaries of the growing state involvement in the welfare of its citizens. They would also participate in the growing post-war consumer affluence, and their aspirations would be more likely to be validated – even if sweets were one of the very last things to come off ration in 1953, and it would be almost a decade before the concept of the 'teenager' as a separate category between child and adult gained wide acceptance, and almost two before the true glory decade of youth, the 'swinging sixties', dawned.

"The day will come when the joybells will ring again throughout Europe, and when victorious nations, masters not only of their foes but of themselves, will plan and build in justice, in tradition, and in freedom . . ."

TO Rt Hon WINSTON'S CHURCHILL, C.H. M.P. Jan 20th, 1940

203

Bibliography

Anderson, Verily. *Spam Tomorrow*. London: Rupert Hart-Davis, 1956.

Boyd, William (ed.). *Evacuation in Scotland: A Record of Events and Experiences*. Bickley, Kent: London University Press, 1944.

Brown, Mike. *A Child's War. Growing Up on the Home Front, 1939–1945*. Stroud, Glos.: Sutton Publishing, 2000.

Brown, Mike. *Evacuees: Evacuation in Wartime Britain, 1939–1945*. Stroud, Glos: Sutton Publishing, 2000.

Burlingham, Dorothy, and Freud, Anna. *Young Children in Wartime: A Year's Work in a Residential Nursery*. London: George Allen and Unwin, 1942.

Calder, Angus. *The People's War*. London: Jonathan Cape, 1969.

Crosby, Travis. L. *The Impact of Civilian Evacuation in the Second World War*. Beckenham: Croom Helm, 1986.

Edom, Robert. *A Great Life if You Don't Weaken*. London: Minerva Press, 2000.

Fethney, Michael. *The Absurd and the Brave. CORB: The true account of the British Government's World War II evacuation of children overseas*. Lewes, Sussex: The Book Guild, 1990.

Field, Geoffrey. 'Perspectives on the Working-Class Family in Wartime Britain, 1939-1945.' In *International Labour and Working-Class History*, no.38, Fall 1990.

Foreman, Michael. *War Boy: A Country Childhood*. London: Puffin, 1991.

Gardiner, Juliet. *'Over Here': GIs in Wartime Britain*. London: Collins and Brown, 1992.

Gardiner, Juliet. *The 1940s House*. London: Channel Four Books, 2000.

Gardiner, Juliet. *Wartime: Britain 1939–1945*. Headline, 2004.

Holman, Bob. *The Evacuation: A Very British Revolution*. Oxford: Lion Publishing, 1995.

Inglis, Ruth. *The Children's War. Evacuation: 1939–1945*. London: Wm Collins, 1989.

Johnson, B.S. (ed.). *The Evacuees*. London: Gollancz, 1968.

Kops, Bernard. *The World Is a Wedding*. London: MacGibbon and Kee, 1963.

Lewis, Peter. *A People's War*. London: Methuen, 1986.

Longmate, Norman. *How We Lived Then. A history of everyday life during the Second World War*. London: Hutchinson, 1971.

Longmate, Norman. *The Doodlebugs: The Story of the Flying Bombs*. London: Hutchinson, 1981.

Parsons, Martin L. *'I'll Take that One': Dispelling the Myths of Civilian Evacuation*. Peterborough: Beckett Karlson, 1998.

Strachey, Mrs St Loe. *Borrowed Children*. London: John Murray, 1940.

The Story of the Mary Datchelor School, 1877–1977. London: Hodder and Stoughton, 1977.

They Were Prepared. London: Boy Scouts' Association, 1942.

Titmuss, Richard L. *Problems of Social Policy*. London: HMSO, 1950.

Turner, Barry, and Rennell, Tony. *When Daddy Came Home: How Family Life Changed Forever in 1945*. London: Hutchinson, 1995.

Wallis, Jill. *A Welcome in the Hillsides? The Merseyside and North Wales Experience of Evacuation: 1939–45*. Wirral, Merseyside: Avid Publications, 2000.

Wicks, Ben. *No Time to Wave Goodbye*. London: Bloomsbury, 1988.

Zweiniger-Bargielowska, Ina. *Austerity in Britain: Rationing, Controls and Consumption, 1939–1955*. Cambridge: Cambridge University Press, 2000.

Acknowledgements and Permissions

I am most grateful to a number of people who have made it both possible and pleasurable to write this book. At the Imperial War Museum my debts start with Angela Godwin who conceptualised the exhibition and encouraged and enabled the book: they continue with her most helpful assistants Gemma Maclagan and Diana Morley. Roderick Suddaby, Keeper of the Department of Documents, has once again proved a mine of information and helpful suggestions, as have his colleagues, Katharine Martin, Amanda Mason and Tony Richards. Nigel Steel drew my attention to a wealth of material, and Penny Ritchie Calder was most helpful as was Emma Crocker in the Photographic Archive, and Margaret Brookes in the Sound Archive, and the staff of the Department of Printed Books. Dr Terry Charman read the manuscript with rigorous attention to detail and great speed and I am, as so often, most grateful for his expertise.

At Piatkus, I am indebted to Alan Brooke for his enthusiasm and support in getting this project off the ground and overseeing its progress, and to the extremely hard work of Alison Sturgeon for making it a reality. At Compendium Simon Forty and Frank Ainscough have made the task as smooth as possible. My thanks, as usual, to my agent Deborah Rogers.

I am also grateful both to the Trustees of the Imperial War Museum and to the individual copyright holders for allowing me access to the collections of papers and recordings held by the IWM and for permission to publish extracts from them.

Department of Documents

The papers of:
J.G. Atherton (88/49/1); Mrs R. Balister (née Mines) (92/9/1); Miss W.J.Beer (02/28/1); Mrs Anne Bowley (née Wallace) (96/26/1); K.W.Brooker (Misc. 240); R.A. Child (97/27/1); Miss V Goddard (Con Shelf); K.F. Gosling (96/31/1); Miss E.L.Helliar (92/49/1); P.J. Holloway (01/31/1); Miss D.M Hoyles (77/50/1); Miss D.E.King (later Mrs Miller) (97/27/1); Mrs. E.H. Kisalia (née Brown) (92/9/1); Michael Mason (96/18/1); Miss S. Mackay (87/23/1); Miss E.B. Mossman (later Mrs Mardon) (97/40/1); Kenneth Muers (97/27/1); Mrs J Nagel (61/40/1); Miss E.M. Paish (later Mrs E.M.Thomson) (Con Shelf); J. C.Phillips (91/47/2); Brian Poole (92/29/1); Mrs F.M.Rollinson (99/66/1); Miss B.L. Roose (89/19/1); Mrs M Trotter (P338); S.R. Turrell (96/18/1); R.A. Weir (88/49/1); Miss L.M. Williams (later Mrs L.M.Hooper) (92/16/1); Miss J.F. Zilva (02/1/1)

Sound Archive

Reginald Baker Acc.no. 006498
Dennis Hayden Acc.no.005266
Ronald McGill Acc. no. 006221
Irene Mead (née Weller) Acc.no. 005343
Harold Shipley Acc.no. 12164
Gwendolen Stewart(née Watts) Acc. no. 334
Mary Walker Whiteman Acc.no. 009730

Mass-Observation Archive

I would like to thank the Trustees of the Mass-Observation Archive, University of Sussex for permission to quote from file reports and topic collections held at the M-O Archive.

File Reports

11 Evacuation report; 17 Toys in wartime; 87 What children think of war; 272 Press and radio notes: inc. items of evacuation of the children from wealthy families; 299 Children and war; 337 Leisure; 367 Leisure; 574 War in December dairies; 1067 Babies in wartime; 1662-3 What your child thinks about the war

Topic Collections

Box 230 Living Through the Blitz. Children in Air Raids
Box 282 Jokes, graffito, toys etc. File 1/E

The Mary Datchelor School Story © The Clothworkers' Company

Index